ROBOTS CAN BRING ADVANTAGES OR DISADVANTAGES

TO OUR SOCIETIES

JOHN LOK

Contents

PREFACE

Introduction

In our societies, how developing and developed countries can apply robotics to improve themselves countries social development to be better, even the best. Can robotic development be applied to help developed and developing noth to improve their societies in success? Can robotic development only be applied to help developed countries to improve their societies more easier to compare developing countries? Is it difficult or it is not possible to apply robotic development to aadvances in artificial intelligence (AI) technology is for the progress in critical areas, such as health, education, energy, economy inclusion, social welfare and the environment. Whether AI can bring positive or negative impaction to influence human job nature change.Thus, it brings this question: Whether (AI) robotic workers can be instead of traditional human workers in these different new markets to bring positive or negative impaction to change human job nature change? In recent years, machines had been used to be human's tasks in the performance of certain tasks related to intelligence , such as aspects of image recognition. Experts also forecast that rapid progress in the field of specialized artificial intelligence will continue. Then, it also brings this question: Does (AI) exceed that of human performance on more and more tasks to replace human jobs? If it is truth, will some of human jobs to be disappeared? (AI) will be instead of human some simple jobs, then unemployment rate to the low skillful and low educated workers will be increased.

Whether (AI) will be raised either production or performance or unemployment to bring human job market more advantages or more disadvantages? In my this book, I shall explain whether (AI) will bring benefits or disadvantages to human job market. I shall give example to let my readers to think how to support my final view point.

Can robtics workers bring what positive or negative influences to office working environment ?Artificial intelligence had been developed to be applied to any service , working aspects, e.g. auto-driven cars. In the future, it may replace manual transport drivers in possible, e.g. non-manual driven tram, train, bus, taxi etc. public transport service. In factory warehouse environment, it can replace some workers to deliver any goods in warehouse. In shopping center service environment, it can replace security to do patrol jobs. In restaurant, it can replace waiter to deliver food to client's table. So, AI will assist or replace any service workers to do any kinds of simple jobs in any working environment in possible future.Final chapter, I shall explain why one organization has excellent facility management strategy, which can help it to prolong or expand long time to stay on mature life cycle stage in possible.

In my this book, I shall let readers to attempt to make judgement whether AI can improve manufacturing efficiency, marketing development, creating jobs, changing public transport to none manual driving public tranport tools and space technological development to assist only developed countries.

PROLOGUE

competitive effort in societies
Can bring global benefit when all
countries are developed countries
1. How Globalization Affects Developed
Countries
Conflicting Globalization Views
● Benefits of globalization
● Drawbacks of globalization
● What Is Globalization?
● Why and how globalization may achieve
when global countries can develop
to become developed countries ?
● Components of Globalization
● The degree to which an organization is globalized and diversified has bearing on the strategies that it uses to pursue greater development and investment opportunities.
● Effect of globalization on developing countries or third world countries
● What influences to the countries like china and India has grown tremendously after globalization.
● Effect of globalization on developed countries when all developing countries can become developed countries
● Development of "Regional economic" will truly help India to build viable economic future for its citizens.
● Regional economies help to reduce domination of developed economies on the developing economies.
    2. Economic growth advantages and disadvantages
● Are economic growth and development worthwhile?
● Economic growth and development of Asia when all or many developing countries can develop to be developed countries
● Model of economy development: The production function how can be influenced to change when many or all developing countries can become developed countries
● How global developed economy influences household expenditure decision?
● How global developed economy influences the labor supply function changes ?
● How global developed economy influences wage rate versus labor leisure

changes?

● Economic development theories: Harrod-Domar theory
    Will developed countries become
developing countries

● Why does illness can cause global economic recession to developed countries p.81-91

● Increasing social crime rate and government assistance may cause developed countries to become developing coutries

● Developed countries lack effort to manufacture cheap products to sell strengths

● Climate change will impact developed countries to continue develop
    Chapter 5
Reasons developed countries need improvement
Why Japan traditional technology needs development p.92-116
Why America needs to build better culture
Why England needs to raise educational level
Why India needs to improve medical technology
Why do developed countries need to continue to learn how to improve new technology
    Chapter 6
Robotic future development how to influence developing and developed countries societies
Electronic vehicle how influences future gas p.117-137
vehicle market life cycle stage experience changes
HOW DESIGNING UNDERGROUND MASS TRANSIT RAILWAY TO BRING PASSENGERS
    Management science solves public transport passenger
queue problem
Waiting Line (Queuing) Models: solution imbalanced taxi
and passenger queue in airport case
    ● Designing transportation system advantages p.138-150
● Underground train transportation needs to
know passenger behaviour reasons
reference
● How to let passengers feel impact of
undergrouund train transport to their working time efficiency
● How underground train MTR can let passengers to feel

catching time reducing .

Artificial Intelligent In Road Transportation
Strategy
How artificial intelligent vehicle may interact intelligent
transportation tools
● Why can (AI) machine learning system main factor to influence driving
consumer individual desires ?
● Non-manual driving transportation tool market development
● Why temperature control can be applied to intelligent transportation
tools
● How technological technology influence intelligent transportation
market development
AI safe immediate response system
Factors influence public transport service industry reaches
life cycle decline stage

How robotic apply to Facility management strategy how assists
organizations to
prolong time to stay on mature life cycle stage
● Facility management influences airport and logistic
employee performance p.151-170
● Facility management assists employees reduce
maintenance service expenditure
● Facility management role in organization
● What is a facility manager's role to provide
quality service to satisfy its user needs?
● Facility management benefits to service
working environment
● Music (FM) environment influence consumer
consumption desire
● Facility management brings departmental benefits
● What is efficient achievement of technological
inputs factor in construction industry
● How organizational facility environment factor influences
new and old employees long term performance
● Facility management how influences employee Psychology to raise
productive efficiency

I

Defining developed and developing countries differences

● What are the developed countries and developing countries characteristics

What factors cause the differences between developed countries and developing countries? Do they have significant unique characteristics to be discovered to influence their differences? I shall attempt to indicate evidences to explain whether these are significant different unique characteristics between any developed countries and developed countries as below:

ON economic measurement aspect, low-and middle income economies are usually referred to as developing economies , and the upper middle income and the high income are referred to as developed countries. So, a developing country also called a less developed country or emerging market, it has a lower gross domestic product(GDP) than developed countries, with a less nature and sophisticated economy. The difference is between developed and developing countries. It may indicate that developed countries refer to the Sovereign (independent) nation/state whose economy has highly progressed and possesses great technological improvement, as compared to other nations.

The countries with low industrialization and low human development indix are formed as developing countries. The World Bank classified the world's economies into four groups, based on Gross National Income per capita: high, upper middle, lower-middle , and low income countries. Least developed countries, landlocked developing countries and small island developing states are all sub-groupings of developing countries. However, it is not ensure that it is only all islands are developing countries, e.g. New Zealand may be one developing country or low developed country also. Experts have said the Guyana has one of the fastest -growing economies in the world.

The unique characteristics differences between developed countries and developing countries. They may include: developing countries are ususally poor, according to the Asian development bank, the major causes of poverty may include: Low economic growth, a week agricultural sector, increased population rates and a high volume of inequality. So, the features of developing countries, their common characteristics may include: low per capita real income, low per capita real income is one of the most defining because amony any developed countries , they may also include highly and lowly developed countries. For example, Norway is the most developed nation in the world. Switzerland is the second developed country in the world, Ireland is the third-most developed country. Then all of these nations may be highly developed countries , e.g. Germany, Hong Kong, China, Australia, Iceland, Sweden. So , it seems that New Zealand may be a lowly developed country to compare above these highly developed countries.

● What factors assist the developing countries to become
developed countries

However, the most developing countries in the world, they may include India, Brazil, China, Argentina is actually considered a developing country and characteristics of developing economies, high population is continue growing. Otherwise, China had began to use methods to discourage Chinese families to born more than one child in order to avoid population continue grows to bring social future burden.

Dependence on primary sector, e.g. Africa and India and New Zealand , they were still depending on main agricutural fruit, rice primary farming industry for themselves main GDP export income source as well as dependence on exports of primary commodities. So, developing countries should need focus on human development, it will remain the main focus of developing countriespost 2015 year. In this regard, the transition of developed countries to equitable and sustainable consumption will make in easier for developinf countries to pursue their human development goals in a more environmental susttainable way.

Hence, human development will may to help developing countries to develop more easily. It is future essential element to assist any one developing countries to be developed countries in success.

The unique characteristics of developing countries include that: Literacy rate is quite low as people are deprived of education facilities, the standard of living in developing countries is normally not very high. Otherwise, developed countries literacy rate is quite high , due to better education ayatem and life expectancy rate is more , due to better standing living. So, in general, the standard of living is very high to developed countries, e.g. UK, US , they have many the low income level or poor people still may have enough money to save in bank and the number of poor people is less in themselves countries, due to definitional discrepancies countries, such as Maxico, Greece and Turkey. India may be nowadays developing countries.

However, there are agrument or disagreement between developed and developing countries. The developed countries say that developing countries must stop burning fossil, fuels and other things that harm the atmosphere. Otherwise, developing countries argue that developed countries have developed by burning the fossil fuels. They say their development will be affected if they stop burning fuels. For Japan example, it is one highly developed country because ir is one of the largest and most developed economies in the world. It has a well-educated, industrious workforce and its large , affluent population makes it is one of the world's biggest consumer markets. Otherwisem New Zealand is not high technological and industrious developed country, it still depends on agricultural fruits, meats export farming industry for main GDP growth source. So, comparison New Zealand and Japan development speed, New Zealand is one lowly developed country. Otherwise, Japan is one highly developed country in nowadays our society. But, the comparison between New Zealand and China, China is still a developing country , but New Zealand may be one lowly developed country to compare China because Chinese government has repeatedly stated that China is the world's largest developing country, despite rapid economic growth over the past four decades. However, according to the 2018 survey, the United States is the world's most powerful country, following countries may include: Japan, Israel, South Korea, Saudi, Arabia, but the safest country may be Iceland because its crime rate is the least. Although, US,

UK may be highly developed countries, but their crime rate may be high position. So, one highly developed country does not represent that it must have the most safest social living environment to let its citizen to feel safe to live. It may be any one highly developed countries themselves failure points. However, environmental factors may also stop a country from developing because some places experience environmental issues, which can present them from developing, examples might be extremee flooding or desertification social factors may also stop a country from developing, e.g. high crime rate, high unemployed rate, low safe living feeling rate, low living standard, they are some parts of the world have issues that are caused by people to influence any countries continue to develop to be one developed country easily. So, all of these factors can assist any one developing country to become developed country.

II

What factors cause developed countries continue developed

What factors cause New Zealand to be developed country
in success
What factors influence New Zealand is still one lowly developed country?
Can New Zealand fight itself country weaknesses to become one highly
developed country? I shall attempt to indicate several evidences to explain
what factors influence New Zealand can not develop to reach mature social
development stage in itself nowadays society are below:
New Zealand is a small population country. It has only 4.8 million . However,
there are many NZ people feel poverty to live. The causes of poverty in
New Zealand. They may include: income inequality, lack of a simple fund
support from government, lack of economic infrastructure, poor access to
education, poor access to healthcase, opinion was evenly diviced on the
primary cause of child poverty in NZ. Forty percent of NZ people said it was
due to economic factors including unemployment, low wages, and rising
living costs, the ever-increasing monthly power bills the the NZ government
won't regulate or gone down.
However, in NZ, poverty is seen as relative, whereby those suffering
deprivation are often struggling to feed their children, living in insecurce
circumstances and unable to enjoy a satisfying social life easily to many
New Zealanders. As a result, many NZ family members' health suffers and

children fail to achieve a sound level of education. IN fact, there is poverty in the midst of prosperity in NZ. There is poverty amidst prosperity: There are around 682,500 people in poverty in this country or one in seven households, including around 220, 000 children .

In general, there are the causes of poverty reasons to any countries, they may include: lack of good jobs / job growth, lack of good education, the second root causes of poverty is a lack of education, a lack of social welfare, weather/ climate change, social injustice, lack of food and water, lack of government support. Although NZ may be belonged to one developed country. But, it is still staying on the lowly developed stage in long time development process. The main factors cause NZ is still one lowly developed country. They may include : lack of good jobs growth in order to let graduates can find good jobs to do and education level can not be improved . What factors cause NZ lacks good job growht and poor education improvement in long time?

In fact, NZ likes many developed countries, its witnessing a transformation in itself economy and employment opportunities. Its traditional exporting sectors , such as dairy, meat, forestry and tourism, remain important drivers of growth. So, NZ's main source of income, they are agricutlural products export, principally meat, dairy products, and fruits and vegetables , crude oil and wood and paper products are also significant. However, the impacts of poverty in NZ, because children in poor communities are three times more likely than the average child to be sick twice as likely to end up in hospital, and sudden unexpected death in infancy rates are more than 6 times higher for infants in the most disadvantaged areas of NZ. These harmful effects run into adulthood in NZ.

What are the most common jobs in NZ? The most popular carre was police officer. SO, when many NZ people hope to seek policeforce jobs. NZ will bring poor job growth development chance to let graduates have plans to develop other professional career in society. Many NZ graduates only consider policeforce jobs, it is one poor social job culture in NZ. However, NZ education is better than America in possible. NZ is definitely superior to the US, in the OECD nations indication, NZ is ranked 3 rd for education quality behinf Finland and Canada, the US ranks about 12 th . Why does NZ still be one lowly developed country in possible, when it can have superior education system?

In fact, NZ ranks highly on most indicators of well-being, but average social level of incomes are low , in general, inequality income were allocated and made NZ economy less developed in the face of shocks, due to low labour productivity factor, low labour productiviey is only partly explained by the farming main industry of the NZ economy and is primarily a consequence of low mulit-factor productivity growth within NZ other industries development, instead of farming industry as well as weak investment on other industries, e.g. technololgical, computer manufacturing , medicine life science drug manufacturing, construction, engineering, e.g. robotic manufacturing etc. different industries development. So, NZ neglects to consider how to develop other industries instead of concentrating on only development on agricultural industry.

However, economic geography is an important factor in NZ's poor productivity performance as the small size and remoteness of the economy diminish its access to global markets, the scale and efficiency of domestic businesses, the level of competition, and the ability to benefit from innovation at the global frontier. All of these many be the main cause weaknesses to NZ countinue development in success.

Moreover, NZ government lacks good policy to support its productivity growth, e.g. lacking to promoting international connections, none removing barriers to fixed capital investment to NZ domestic any industries development, instead of agricultural industry, accessing benefits of agricultural industry, accessingg benefits by improving urban planninf, enhancing competition and increasing investment in innovation and intangibles.

Hence, poor productivity technological improvement may be on main factor to cause NZ productivity growth is poor. It is main reason to cause NZ is one lowly developed country in long time, because global highly developed countries concerned high technological productivity is expected to be the main driver of income source , in particular via investment in technology and knowledge-based capital. So, any highly developed countries began to believe that economic growth from productivity improvements contributes to welfare through increasing the worker individual income that can be earned from each hour worked, providing individuals with the option to work lesss or consume moew job and service. Hence , NZ lacks high technological productivity improved to let any one talent NZ person can have chance to use his / her talent knowledge to do high technological jobs in order to attribute NZ society and to earn high hour income. NZ is only developing agricultural industry nowadays. SO, agricultural jobs wil be common jobs in NZ developed country. Hence, low technolgical productive improvement may be main factor to influence NZ to be one lowly developed country in long time.

What factors influence US and UK continue development
Why do US and US be a developed country? It has a high-income economy and a very high human development index rating. Ranking 13 th in the world. Today, the UK , US remains one of the world's great powers with considerable economc, cultural , military, scientific, technological and political influence internationally. Why are UK and US econome so strong? It's quality of life is generally considered high, and the economy is quite diversified . The sectors that contibute must be the US, UK 's GDP are services, manufacturing, construction and tourism . Moreover, UK and US are the world's largest economy by normimal GDP and net wealth and they are the second largest by purchasing power. Themselves nations's economy is fueled by natural resources, a well-developed and high productivity.
It seems that UK and US have a mixed economic development, developed through free market and global economy , which are regulated by their governments to prevent market failure easily.

III

What Factors Influence Social Development Speed

What factors cause why some countries can develop rapidly ? What factors cause some countries develop slowly? It would be hard to find a more fundamental conept for the social development and human development. The social development science is about human societies how we develop, so we had better have some idea to explain how and why what factors cause some countries can develop rapidly , e.g. US, UK, or what factors cause some countries can develop slowly, e.g. China, India. The reaons that there has been a question about the development speed to any countries , it has been an active and influential movement to insist that this was a human social development question. Why does Inida has many years history, otherwise, US has less many years histroy, what factors influence US can develop more rapidly to compare Inida? Even, India seems to be one developing country in nowadays society.

From sociobiology to social development psychology

What factors to India is facing to influence it can not succeed to develop to be highly developed country easily? Human cognitive mechanisms evolved in the Pleistocene, the period from about 2 million years ago, about 10,000 years ago, the end of the last Ice age, MOtivating this choice is the thought that substantial periods of development time are required for significant evolutionary change, such as social need change, family need change, country need change. Much of Evolutinnary psychology has consisted of reflection on the different countries changing conditions that might have obtained during this perios, and the human development behaviors what would have been most favoured by natural selection given those conditions. First of all to what influences human feels we need to develop, a lot of human behavior has roots that are far more ancient. Sociability , for instance, is not a uniquely human attribute. But significant changes in the nature of human sociality are evident over historical periods of tens or hundrends of years, presumably because they are due to cultural improvement, or raising human cultural quality , so our cultural improvement psychology influences why some countries can not develop rapidly, such as India does not consider itself Indian cultural level needs to raise significantly. Otherwise, US condiers itself American cultural level need to raise significantly. So, this cultural development reason may explain why India is still one developing country, although, its has many years history to compare US.

Social Development Psychology

Another important point about social development issus, it is the environmental factor, it is one picture to influence why some countries develop rapidly , but some countries still develop slowly. I don nor need to pursue that argument , since the focus will remain on the human development case, and no one could suppose that the social enviroment that human create for, among the other things, the production of new human social behaviors, is simply a consequence of genetically determined human behavior. For example, American hopes that it can create many talent people to help itself country to develop, so talent people development environment need can influence US can have many talent people to create to help itself country to develop to be highly developed country in short time, e..g. space science, life science etc.

I wished to emphasize particularly the ability of cultural evolution to transform the social development history to different countries issus. It seems clear that humans have learned in quite recent time to construct a remarkably social changing environment for the development for their young. So, any countries their future development, they must depend on how many talent young people, they can create. It is very important issue to influence any one country to develop to be one high developed or low developed or developing country. For that reason their introduction should be seen as representing major cultural improvemernt and social environment factors to influence any countries their future development speed. For this simple example, many further illustrate the point, they indicate that the mobile phone did not exist when I was a child. In fact, it is for hardly more than a decade that it has been for everyday life in developed countries. Ans whereas it may seem only more or less need for people of my generation, for those aged, say 10 to 20 , age, it is as unthinkable to deprived of one's phone as to wander the streets stark naked. Most teenagers move through the would, when this smart phone technological development, it can influence any one feels that it is essential product to our daily need. It is one cultural improvement factor example , it can explain why global many people feel smart phones are essential product to satisfy us need. It is not, therefore, merely behavior that has changed for those who have grown up with the mobile phone, but the social environment can bring indirect to influence any one , even old age feels smart phone need, when old age people can contact many young people , they must own least one smart phone for personal use. So, cultural improvement and social environment changing need both factors can influence any one country may make development decision in short time or long time, when the country people feel that they have urgent social and cultural improvement changing need rapidly.

IV

What are the differences between developing and developed countries

I shall explain the difference between developed and developing countries characteristics as below:

Countries are divided into two major categories by the United Nations, which are developed countries and developing countries. The classification of countries is based on the economic status such as GDP, GNP, per capita income, industrialization, the standard of living, etc. Developed Countries refers to the soverign state, whose economy has highly progressed and possesses great technological infrastructure, as compared to other nations. The countries with low industrialization and low human development index are termed as developing countries. Developed Countries provides free, healthy and secured atmosphere to live whereas developing countries, lacks these things.

The characteristics between developing and developed countries may include as below:

Developed countries means that a country having an effective rate of industrialization and individual income is known as Developed Country. Otherwise, developing Country is a country which has a slow rate of industrialization and low per capita income. Developed countries have low unemployment and poverty, developing countries have usually high unemployment and poverty. developed countries have low infant mortality rate, death rate and birth rate is low while the life expectancy rate is high. Otherwise, developing countries have high infant mortality rate, death rate and birth rate, along with low life expectancy rate. Developed countries have better living conditions and high standard of living, but developing countries have bad living conditions and low standard of living. Developing countries have high GDP from industrial sector income source, otherwise, developed countries have high GDP income from service sector income source. Developing countries have high industrial growth. Otherwise, developed countries, they rely on the developed countries for their growth. Developed countries have high equal of distribution of income, otherwise, developing countries have high unequal of distribution of income. Finally, developed countries have effectively utilized to factors of production, otherwise, developing countries have ineffectively utilized to factors of production. Overall , any thing of developed countries are better than developing countries in nowadays societies.

Between developed and developing countries, one can identify a variety of differences. This differentiation of countries, as developed and developing, is used to classify countries according to their economic status based on per capita income, industrialization, literacy rate, living standards, etc.

● What are Developed Countries?

They have usually these similar characteristics as below:

(1) Developed countries have industrial growth and enjoy flourishing economy. Developed countries experience marked development and growth in the areas such as transportation, business, and education. Developed countries are characterized by a low death rate and low birth rate as well. There is usually a very small gap between the two rates in developed countries.

(2) Developed countries are not characterized by shortcomings. They are well-developed in all fronts and are served well by water supplies, amenities, educational institutions, health care concerns. This is because of the fact that people are endowed with awareness about every possible aspect relating to human existence. The absence of shortcomings in the developed countries is possibly due to the fact there is a low birth rate in these countries. Nutrition is available in plenty to mothers and infants in developed countries.

● What are Developing Countries?

They have usually these similar characteristics as below:

(1) Developing countries depend on the developed countries for help to establish their industries. They have only begun to taste the growth of the economy. Developing countries are in the beginning stages of development in the areas of education, business, and transportation.

(2) Developing countries are characterized by many shortcomings. These shortcomings include less awareness regarding matters relating to health, poor amenities, shortage in water supply, shortcoming in the area of medical supply, a higher rate of birth rate. The most important and worrying factor in the developing countries is the factor of poor nutrition. Poor nutrition to both mothers and infants is the main concern in the developing countries. Due to high birth rates, the probability of natural diseases is more in developing countries. Hence, the death rates are also eventually high in developing countries. However, since natural diseases increase by high rates in the developing countries, they will have a short population doubling time. In the case of developing countries, there is usually a big gap between the birth rate and the death rate. Infant mortality factor is influenced by the development factor of countries. A developing country for that matter would have higher infant mortality than a developed country.

Overall, economists will differ their different characteristcs from these several aspects as below:

Developed countries display a high level of development. Developing countries: Developing countries display a lower development in different areas such as industrialization, human capital, etc. Developed countries have industrial growth. Developing countries depend on the developed countries for help to establish their industries. Developed countries enjoy flourishing economy. Developing countries begin to taste the growth of the economy. Developed countries experience marked development and growth in the areas such as transportation, business, and education. Developing countries are in the beginning stages of development in the areas of education, business, and transportation. Developed countries are characterized by a low death rate and low birth rate as well. There is usually a very small gap between the two rates in developed countries. In developing countries there is usually a big gap between the birth rate and the death rate. Hence, in overall, any aspects are worse, slow growth to developing countries compare to developed countries.

● What are general their GDP difference

Developed Countries:

A developed nation is one that has a very high rank in industrial advancement, constructs its economy in light of innovation and assembling rather than agribusiness. The variables of production, for example, human and regular assets are completely used bringing about an increment underway and utilization which prompts a very high rank in per capita salary. A nation with a more Human Development Index (HDI) is viewed as a developed nation. It not just measures the financial improvement and GDP of a nation additionally its instruction and future.

Developing Countries:

A developing nation is those having a way of life or level of modern advancements well beneath that conceivable with money related or specialized guide; a nation that is not yet exceptionally industrialized. A country having less utilization of resources and low income per capita which leads to low GDP of a country.

● Developed VS Developing Countries will have different development or growth speed to compare as below:

?Industrial Economies:

In developed countries, economy depends on industrial sector instead of agriculture sector. There is more development in industrial sector. In developing countries, mostly economy depends on agriculture sector and they are moving toward industrialization.

?Citizens:

In developed countries, citizens and well off and rich. In developing countries, proportion of rich citizens is very low.

?Unemployment:

In developed countries, there is no such issue of unemployment. They provide many employment opportunities to the citizens. In developing countries, issue of unemployment is there and it affects the economy of country very badly.

?Education:

The growth rate in education sector is very high in developed countries and they have best education systems. Whereas the growth rate of developing countries in education sector is low as compare to developed countries. While developing countries are following the education system of developed countries to achieve the standard.

?Technological advantages:

In developed countries, every place is full with technological advancements and they always try to make it better. In developing countries, there are many undeveloped rural areas and even urban sector have less technological advancements.

?Roads:

Developed countries have a very sound infrastructure by having better roads, railway tracks, airports etc. Developing countries don't have a sound infrastructure as compare to developed countries.

?Government:

There exists stable government in developed countries so that they make effective and reliable policies for better economic development. Developing countries have unstable governments and mostly try to following the policies made by developed countries.

?Health care:

In developed countries, good and better facilities for health have been provided to citizens. In developing countries, health care facilities are not so good and acceptable.

?Resources:

In developed countries, the natural and human resources are fully and efficiently consumed. In developing countries, many of the natural resources are still untouched and others resources are also not fully utilized.

?Income:

There is a high level of income as per citizen living in developed country so that they have high GDP and GNP. Developing countries have low level of income as per citizen living in country with unequal distribution of income as that have low GDP and GNP.

?High Human Development Index (HDI):

In developed countries, there are best education systems and better health care and high income level so this leads to high value and ranking of HDI. In developing countries, there are low income level and fewer facilities for health care and low rates of education so this leads to low or middle ranking in HDI.

?Life expectancy:

In developed countries, due to better health care the life expectancy has been increased and they have low birth rates as well as low death rates. In developing countries, life expectancy is not so high but has high rates of birth and death due to less facilities and education.

?Water and food supply:

In developed countries, safe and clean water is supplied with plentiful supply of food items and good housing condition. In developing countries, dirty and unsafe water is supplied with less reliable food items and poor condition of houses.

In conclusion, all our daily necessary need and social need to developing countries growth will be worse to compare developed countries in our nowadays societies.

● How to measure the difference between developed and developing countries ?

The measurement factors between developed and developing countries may include as below:

(1) GDP factor

The classification of a country does not only depend on its income but also on other factors that affect how their citizens live, how their economies are integrated into the global system, and the expansion and diversification of their export industries. A developed country is one that has a high level of industrial development, bases its economy on technology and manufacturing instead of agriculture. The factors of production such as human and natural resources are fully utilized resulting in an increase in production and consumption which leads to a high level of per capita income. A country with a high Human Development Index (HDI) rating is considered a developed country. It not only measures the economic development and GDP of a country but also its education and life expectancy. A developed country's citizens enjoy a free and healthy existence.

(2) Industralization or Commercial aspect factor

The term "developed country" is synonymous to "industrialized country, post-industrial country, more developed country, advanced country, and first-world country." The United Kingdom, France, Germany, Canada, Japan, Switzerland, and the United States of America are only a few of those considered as developed countries. A developing country, on the other hand, is one that has a low level of industrialization.

It has a higher level of birth and death rates than developed countries. Its infant mortality rate is also high due to poor nutrition, shortage of medical services, and little knowledge on health. The citizens of developing countries have a low to medium standard of living because their per capita income is still developing, and their technological capacity is still being developed. There is also an unequal distribution of income in developing countries, and their factors of production are not fully utilized. Developing countries are also referred to as third-world countries or least-developed countries.

Countries are categorized according to their economic development. The

United Nations classifies countries as developed, developing, newly industrialized or developed, and countries in transition such as Kazakhstan, Kyrgyztan, Turkmenistan, and the former USSR. The World Bank classifies countries according to their GNI per capita income: low income ($995 or less) and lower middle income ($996-$3,945); as developing countries with an upper middle income ($3,946-$12,195); and high income (above $11,906) as developed countries.

(3) The country citizen living of standard level

The classification of a country does not only depend on its income but also on other factors that affect how their citizens live, how their economies are integrated into the global system, and the expansion and diversification of their export industries. A developed country is one that has a high level of industrial development, bases its economy on technology and manufacturing instead of agriculture. The factors of production such as human and natural resources are fully utilized resulting in an increase in production and consumption which leads to a high level of per capita income. A country with a high Human Development Index (HDI) rating is considered a developed country. It not only measures the economic development and GDP of a country but also its education and life expectancy. A developed country's citizens enjoy a free and healthy existence.

The term "developed country" is synonymous to "industrialized country, post-industrial country, more developed country, advanced country, and first-world country." The United Kingdom, France, Germany, Canada, Japan, Switzerland, and the United States of America are only a few of those considered as developed countries.

A developing country, on the other hand, is one that has a low level of industrialization. It has a higher level of birth and death rates than developed countries. Its infant mortality rate is also high due to poor nutrition, shortage of medical services, and little knowledge on health. The citizens of developing countries have a low to medium standard of living because their per capita income is still developing, and their technological capacity is still being developed. There is also an unequal distribution of income in developing countries, and their factors of production are not fully utilized. Developing countries are also referred to as third-world countries or least-developed countries.

In conclusion, the measurement factors to decide whether the country is either developing or developed country. The factors depend on whether:

whether the developed country is a country that has a high level of industrialization and per capita income while a developing country is a country that is still in the early stages of industrial development and has a low per capita income , whether the citizens of a developed country enjoy a free, healthy, and affluent existence while citizens of developing countries do not, whether the developed countries are also known as industrialized, advanced, and first-world countries while developing countries are also known as underdeveloped, least developed, and third-world countries. For example, The United States of America, Canada, Switzerland, Belgium, and France are examples of developed countries while India, Malawi, Honduras, the Philippines, and Rwanda are examples of developing countries as well as the infant mortality, birth, and death rates of developing countries are also higher compared to that of developed countries.

Why and how developed countries need
assist developing countries to develop

I think that we should help developing nations, But only to an extent. If we keep, And keep on giving them needs they will start to rely on foreign aid. I think charities are enough, But if the developing countries really need help then we give them help. But not too much, Basically they need to do something themselves and stop relying and take their own action. In exchange for our help maybe they could give us a bit of natural resources? Developing countries may need to be assisted, They may include these reasons:

● Global resource is shortage to allocate unfair challenge

Nowadays, global resources are not equally distributed in different countries. Thus, there are those who belong to the developed nations while there are others that belong to developing countries. With these unequal distribution, it is significant that developed countries must do their part in helping those who belong to the underprivileged sector. It is true that rich countries have their own problems to worry with; Can we introduce aquaponics in developing countries when they don't have the resources that first world countries have? In many areas, there is no electricity available that is needed for many aquaponics systems; developing countries require simplicity, reliability, and freedom from the need of grid powerhowever, it is still their responsibility to help the developing countries people need to solve resource can not be allocated fair problem, such as Afria is one developing country, many people are drinking drink water, due to drought , so they will not feel health and they will feel sick , even die. It is one example of natural resource of clean water shortage challenge to Afica. So, developed country, e.g. US , it has responsibilty to help African to drink clean water because clean water is allocated to supply to America people to drink in preference, due to global clean water supply is decreasing, but human number is increasing and clean water demand will also increase. If clean water is only supplied to US people to drink , even other developed countries people , they can drink the most clean water. The reason is because Africa people is poor or dirty or low education level or it is one developing country etc. factors to influence many African can not often drink any clean water. It is very unfair to this developing country.

In 2010, there were 925 million hungry people in the world; 19 million in developed countries, 37 million in Near East and North Africa, 53 million in Latin America and the Caribbean, 239 Million in Sub-Saharan Africa, and 578 million in Asia and the Pacific. This means that approximately 1 in 7 people are hungry. Protein- energy malnutrition is the most lethal form of malnutrition/hunger. It is a lack of calories and protein; protein is necessary for key bodily functions including provision of essential amino acids and the development and maintenance of muscles. Bringing aquaponics into third world countries would help prevent this problem by providing fish as a main source of protein. Poor nutrition is the cause or partial cause for at least half of the 10.9 million child deaths each year.

The number of hungry people has increased since 1997 due to three main problems: 1) neglect of agriculture relevant to very poor people by governments and international agencies; 2) worldwide economic crisis and 3) increase in food prices. Children who are poorly nourished suffer up to 160 days of illness each year. Malnutrition affects about 32% of children in developing countries. More than 70% of malnourished children live in Asia. Undernourished pregnant women in developing countries leads to 1 out of 6 infants born with low birth weight; this means higher neonatal death rates, increased occurrences of learning disabilities, mental retardation, poor health, blindness, and premature death. There is enough food to provide everyone in the world with 2, 720 kilocalories per person per day, however many people don't have the land to grow or the money to buy the food they need for themselves and their children. 1 out of 3 people in developing countries are affected by vitamin and mineral deficiency.

So, I feel that aid has diverse results. It can both harm as well help development. Rich countries might be sidetracked in terms of focusing on programs that will spur development. Asian and African nations should create long-term plans that will reduce the dependency on aid, while rich countries should transition from traditional methods of giving support in new ways. Rich countries still argue on the premise that they cannot afford aid or that they are being over-generous. The main idea here is not that they are questioning the aid itself, but the development project. Rich countries must be on the poor countries aid as these people from poor nations face injustice and hardships that are often caused or increased by the programs and decision of rich nations themselves.

However, giving aid is not really an act of generosity. Aid purchases things that donors desire. These might include political support in exchange for the "goodies" that the donor has provided. Rich countries must show support to the poor by abiding on the social, environmental aspects. It can also include adapting to climate change by changing one's own consumption. Another is to accept fairer trade rules. Moreover, rich countries can show true generosity by undergoing changes in the manner of living for the past few decades. It would be fair that rich countries believe they are being generous when they give out dole outs or loose change when poor people around the globe are trying to live on a few basics while living under the system that rich countries have developed. It is a reality that there are also poor people in rich countries that are undergoing tough times. However, it is not ethical to withdraw support from people abroad who are more underprivileged just because there are poor people in rich countries that need help as well.

In fact, many argue that the poor countries that rich countries provide financial aid are doing better economically. It is possible that these countries are growing and catching up with the standard of living. Say for example, the annual income of India might have greatly improved. However, when one divides that with the whole population, each Indian just obtains $3 or less per day. This issue requires obtaining the correct facts not only on financial aid, but on the act of generosity in this world. Rich countries do have a responsibility of giving to those developing country people's living need because they can enjoy any benefits in preference when resource is shortage and global need is also increasing in nowadays societies.

● Some developed countries have obligation to help developing countries

The rich have an obligation to help poor countries who were exploited by their colonial rulers. The United States had a head start with its vast natural resources. But many countries in Europe, such as Britain, became rich due to their colonial reign in Asia. They expanded their empire to include poor, resource-rich nations in Asia. They exploited the region's cheap labour, with workers getting little in return for their hard work. For Hong Kong , developing country and UK developed country. UK had obligation to help this developing country, HK before 1997.

Hong Kong was different though. Britain ruled Hong Kong for more than 150 years and I think both sides benefited. Today, the city is an international financial centre with a strong economy. But some countries did not benefit from colonial rule. For another example, IBM founder , Bill and Melinda Gates set up the Gates Foundation to help poor countries. We take a lot of things for granted. This cannot go on. A spirit of give-and-take is essential for world harmony. Developed countries may not be bound by law to help poor nations, but they have the responsibility - and the power - to do so.

However, developed countries should help less developed ones. But whether this is an obligation is a matter for debate. I believe the government of a country should be responsible for the well-being of its people. It is wrong to allow outsiders to influence the development of a country. This could lead to serious problems.

A developed country faces various difficulties when choosing who to help. First, its choice could leave a lot of people unhappy and damage its relationship with other countries. Second, allowing foreigners to have a significant influence on a nation could lead to negative consequences. Some donors do not have the best intentions. They could use their power for their own advantage. This could lead to corruption and financial loss in the less developed country. Third, a developing nation may become dependent on foreign aid. And some donors might charge a hefty interest for their financial assistance. This could pose a bigger headache than not receiving aid at all. Hence, rich countries have to be careful when helping poor nations. It involves a lot of politics so the rich have the right to choose the recipient and ensure the aid does not get into the wrong hands.

● Rich countries have responsibilites to assist global economy development or balance economy development

When global economy is unbalance developing. It will bring the damage of kindly cooperation relationship , e.g. export and import business activities to develop our global economy in success. For example, China and America themselve trade war will cause these both countries' GDP export and import income loss, even global economy will be recession. So, rich country, such as US has responsibility to assist developing country, such as

Afria, China, Korea, Taiwan to help them to raise business competive effort and bring long term export and import business cooperation and create many factory jobs to China, Korea, Africa, Taiwan factory workers. Then, they can build kindly business cooperative relationship to bring global economy benefit in long term. Then, our global economy development will succeed more easily.

The first rational basis behind donating to poor countries is the notion that all men are equal. Some may radically oppose this concept, noting that their countries should solely invest its own efforts to remedy impoverished sectors of the population. Given the spread of poverty and homelessness, some have arrived to the conclusion that aiding other countries is not in our best interest. However, this could not be further from the truth. As member of the human race, we all occupy an equitable status as global citizens, and nothing can detract from this truth. Centralise your focus on the relative needs of your nation disregards the ailing needs of the developing world.

The second consideration simply poses the question of why not? Although wealthier, developed countries are plagued by their own respective incidences of poverty and lack of resources, developing countries suffer greatly, in terms of their accessibility to medical aid, vaccines, clean water, and a number of other amenities that are gravely understated in importance. With this said, we must venture beyond the bounds of our own comfort zones, and aid other countries because we are lavished with such a bounty in resources ourselves. Another indispensable benefit of aiding impoverished countries. Foreign diplomacy can significantly aid the national security of any nation. And providing aid to a poor county can ultimately benefit us, improving our perception in their eyes, a cultivating a certain level of civility and coexistence that breeds peace, instead of war. The fewer enemies that a particular nation has, the better.

The final reason is simple. We should empathize with other human beings. Every day, countless children succumb to curable disease, malaria and a number of other pathogens that could easily be treated with outside aid. Both children and adults are sold into slavery and trafficked around the world. Of course, the lingering issue of starvation is a palpable one that still plagues the world today. With this said, we should uphold a noble standard that permits foreign aid for this very reason. One often hears the argument that it is all very well to preach equity but given the planetary emergency the world faces from the threat of climate change we must set aside the equity principle in the interests of humanity as a whole. This is a wholly specious and self serving argument. It reflects the sense of entitlement to an affluent lifestyle, based on energy intensive production and consumption, while denying the even modest aspirations of people in developing countries.

For example, global climate changes to warmth challenge , it can cause developing countries people their health to be poor. In a densely interconnected and globalised world, it will be impossible to maintain islands of prosperity in an ocean of poverty and deprivation. It is not that developing countries are claiming the right to spew as much carbon as possible into the atmosphere without regard to the health of the planet. As the main victims of climate change– the impacts of which they are already suffering – they have a much bigger stake in dealing with this challenge. They are, in fact, doing much more than most developed countries, to adopt energy frugal methods of growth, conserving energy, promoting renewable power and limiting waste within the limits of their own resources.

Why and how developing countries people's poor health issue , it may influence developed countries businessmen income ? I shall indicate Africa , developing example , if African are health, then this country will have many workers to assist or help US businessmen to manufacture many products to sell to different countries in short time. If US businessmen hope to pay the low wage to reduce their long time expenditure, Afrian must need have health to do any hard jobs in factories. If US businessmen only feel Chinese workers can help them to do any low wage jobs in factories, when China have many new businesses develop to pay better wages to employ themselves Chinese workers. Then, many Chinese workers may choose to help themselves China employers to do the factory jobs to replace US employers. So, if US can help many African have health to work, it may bring uncounted long time benefits to US businesses. Hence, such as this case, it explains why rich people need to help developing countries to solve health challenge.

Methods developing countries can become developed countries

● Main industries aspects need to develop

How can developing countries develop to be developed countries in success? What the difficulties to them , that they will need to solve in this development process ? In today's sophisticated society,people of the developing countries are still fighting for their basic righs such a better healthcare,proper education and a sound source of income.While the governments of the underdeveloped countries are struggling to improve the living standards of their people,I believe that contribution by richer nations should be more in this regard. To begin,all human beings should help each other.Govenments of richer nations can take many steps to improve the living standard of the poorer naions. I shall indicate these aspects that they need to concentrate on solving in order to achieve developed countries in success as below:

(1) Healthcare development

Firstly,in the field of healthcare,developed countries can support he underdeveloped in many ways.They can send their expert doctors to train the medical staff in the developing countries.Also,they can open free medical camps in the selected areas of poor countries.In this way free medical advice could be given.Such camps can also start health awarness compaigns to make people aware of unhealthy lifetyle. Moreover, experts from the developed countries can also help with the vaccination programmes in the developing countries.This will led to decrease in infant mortality rate.

(2) Educational development

Secondly,assistance in the field of education should be provide to the poorer nations.The developed countries can provide funds to open new schools and polytechnic institutions.These will not only increase the literacy rate,but will also provide vocational education.Furthermore,the rich governments should provide the students of poor countries an oportunity to study in the prestigious institutions by giving scholarships.This will promote poor people to gain higher education.

(3) Promoting free trade development

Finally,rich nations should help to improve the economy of poor countries.This can be done by promoting free trade.This wil reduce barriers to international trade such as tariff,import quotas and export fee and will help to lift the developing countries out of poverty. To conclude,if we want to live in a beter world with peace and harmony,we should always help each other.Therefore,I believe that richer nations should help the poor countries in all the fields.

● The challenges are needed to solve in development process

During the development process, they developing countries will need to solve these challenges, the developing or underdeveloped countries (as they were earlier named) are poor due to them having the following common characteristics as below:

The developing countries may have these social challenges , they need to solve , such as :

(1) On social medical aspect

Closed economy/State Controlled economy or practice of socialism (which is in practice -one man/one party dictatorship). Low levels of literacy and esp. female literacy (less than 75% female literacy). Low health and HDI indicators (corresponding to the literacy levels). Low per capita income. High incidence of corruption, nepotism and kleptocracy.

The following is the path chosen by most of the former "low income/under developed/poor nations" to become developed (Germany & Japan post WW2, South Korea, Taiwan, Brazil, South Africa and China - some are still in process)- Economically liberal but politically/socially conservative regimes. Immense government spending (Keynesian economics) on - Infrastructure (Roads, Schools, Bridges, Ports, Airports, Power Plants, Hospitals and primary health centers etc).

(2) On international trade social aspect

Opening up the economy to international trade and foreign investments. Export oriented manufacturing practices, wherein the bulk of the population which was in the primary sector (agriculture, animal husbandry and mining etc) shifts to the secondary sector (manufacturing) and experiences corresponding increase in wages/income.

Application of procedures and rule of law on a gradual basis from the earlier arbitrariness which reigned supreme. The first step, in my view, is to make sure to have an honest and capable government that are committed to the development of the country and to the welfare of all people in the country. It is, in fact, the most difficult step to start with. Once we have a good and capable government, it is not so difficult to figure out or implement all steps necessary to make the country developed and prosper. On the other hand, having a corrupt, incapable, in other words, not only dishonest, but also stupid and foolish government means losing everything, no matter how abundance resource your country has, or how much foreign assistance and aids your country receives.

However, some economists believe that they are not "developing", but MAINTAINED IN PERMANENT UNDERDEVELOPMENT on purpose. Market, same as everything, functions in 3D, the 3rd is the income strata. The "progress" is not for all the strata. Every upper stratum solves its own problems at expenses of pushing the next inferior one downwards (vertically) or over the edge (horizontally). Spend a few minutes on a search engine and you realize that the term "first world" is meaningless when referring to economic development. For example, Ireland, Switzerland and Sweden are examples of third world countries. A first world nation is one that allied with NATO as opposed to the Soviet Union during the Cold War.

(3) On solving social poverty aspect

Poverty is the default state of man. Knowledge is what allows us to go beyond our physical and cognitive limitations. With knowledge you can create technology that makes our lives better. At a base level, developing nations need a smaller percentage of their populations working in sustenance farming. This could be achieved by increases in farming productivity which would allow other people to specialize in making other goods and providing other services. Essentially creating more wealth.

Uaually, developing countries lack enough farming technology, they can't specialize in something other than sustenance farming if 80% of your population farms with oxen instead of machines. This is where knowledge comes in play. Many developing nations have rich natural resources and commodities they just don't have the knowledge necessary to turn it into something useful.

To summarize in one word what is necessary for a developing nation to become a developed one it is knowledge. Any one developing countries need to answer these questions, before they decide how to solve these social challenges in their development process as below:

What developing country will become the next developed nation? Why do they are developing countries ? How can they develop to be developed countries ? How long will it take for every country in the world to become developed? What is the way to develop a country? Which countries are likely to be developed countries soon?

For example, Brazilians is one developing country, because this country has high crime rate and poor rate is high and inflation is high. These are its social problems. As soon as hyperinflation and out-of-control crime was solved, Brazilians brought their money back to Brazil. The starting point for Brazilians is patriotism and nostalgia. Even with all the problems of corruption, taxes, bureaucracy and poor infrastructure if given a chance to make real money within the country a Brazilian will leave better opportunities in the US. So, Brazilians need to solve these social problems if this country hope to become one developed country in success. The easiest way to develop is: when each and every person decides to learn as much as possible, and decides to behave like civilized persons, who have total respect for all other persons' physical and patrimonial integrity. It's that easy and simple. But, often, the easiest things in life are the most difficult to learn.

● What a developing country should do to be a developed one?

The countries that developed the fastest often had the longest paths. If you compensate for that fact, then it becomes obvious that economic freedom is both necessary and sufficient. In particular, countries should avoid: socialism, i.e. collectivization of the means of production expropriation, i.e. robbing foreign investors of their properties autarchy, i.e. cutting all international trade. The less countries engage in these, the faster they develop.

● How can a developing country become a developed country?

Well, you could study economic history and learn how the present developed countries attained their present positions. There are also several examples in real time: look at how China and India are moving their countries from third world countries to developed economies. Two other interesting examples: Several African countries are using primarily cell phone techologies for communication and bypassing the infrastructure requirements for hardline technology. Ireland is well know to have been deforested when it's forests were harvested for the coal and fuel requirements of industrializing.

● Developed Countries need to help Developing Countries to increase their competitive effort in societies

IMPROVEMENTS IN HEALTH, EDUCATION AND TRADE ARE ESSENTIAL FOR THE DEVELOPMENT OF POORER NATIONS. HOWEVER,THE GOVERNMENTS OF RICHER NATIONS SHOULD TAKE MORE RESPONSIBILITY FOR HELPING THE POORER NATIONS IN SUCH AREAS. Eliminate political tension by encouraging participation of all in the political, constitutional and economic processes. I recommend developed countries, such as US, UK can help developing countries to develop in sucess in these several aspects:

-Invest in infrastructure, education and health care.
-Encourage rural agriculture by providing agricultural inputs
and raising earned incomes.
-Raise levels of literacy
-Encourage the modern sectors of banking, manufacturing, retail,
and extractive industries,
-Provide adequate sanitation and clean water

-Open the countries to direct foreign investments

-Remove trade barriers to exports and imports.

-Reduce dependency on single sectors that is diversification .

Can bring global benefit when all

countries are developed countries

1. How Globalization Affects Developed Countries

There are three perspective of globalization. Which are as : The Hyper globalist perspective: This says that economies are becoming Denationalized due to this government will lose it influence over the trade within its border. It will have both good and bad effects. The Skeptical perspective: it is kind based on myth that globalization will not help the under develop country as they do not perform a greater role in flow of trade and services in the global economy.

I assume that future one day, all countries can become developed countries. The globalization development effect will be caused by our global successful development. Does it means that globalization can only bring benefits ? I shall explain that when all countries can developed successfully. Globalization ought not only bring benefits to our global societies as below: Globalization brings people and businesses together through the international exchange of money, ideas, and culture. However, some critics say it adversely affects developed countries. Opinions exist on both sides of the globalization debate. Proponents claim lower opportunity costs, producing positive growth, and reduced market volatility. At the same time, opponents decry the reduction of domestic job growth, cost of mismanagement to countries and the world, and the stagnation of wages.

Conflicting Globalization Views

U.S. President Donald Trump, for example, has been very vocal on his views of globalization and has taken a protectionist stance when it comes to free trade under agreements like the North American Free Trade Agreement (NAFTA), calling for higher taxes on imports and fewer multinational trade agreements. He has also increased tariffs on foreign goods to discourage their importation and use. No matter how much economists are quick to extol the universal benefits of globalization, some politicians and other economist demonize globalization as a force that takes away domestic jobs. These conflicting viewpoints have created a maelstrom of opinions and policies across developed countries that range from extreme protectionism through trade barriers, like President Trump's example, to complete openness.

From an economic standpoint, globalization is typically defined as the increase in the global trade of goods, services, capital, and technology. This growth in trade has been especially acute between developed countries like the United States and emerging markets, such as China. There are many factors behind the increase in global trade. European devastation after World War I and II helped to jumpstart America and an industrial superpower and exporter. Lower transportation costs have reduced the costs of trade, technologies have eliminated some barriers altogether, and liberal economic policies have helped lower political barriers to trade. While cost reductions have helped accelerate trade, the largest driver behind global trade is supply-demand economics and the desire to increase consumption on the part of both importers and exporters.

Benefits of globalization

The core benefit of globalization is the comparative advantage—that is, the ability of one country to produce goods or services at a lower opportunity cost than other countries. While the idea seems simple on the surface, it quickly becomes counterintuitive when examined more deeply. The theory suggests that two countries capable of producing two commodities at different costs can benefit the most by exporting the good where the comparative advantage exists. For example, a developing country may have a comparative advantage in producing cement, and the United States may have a comparative advantage in producing semiconductors. While the U.S. may be able to produce cement more efficiently than the developing country, the U.S. would still be better off focusing on semiconductors because of its comparative advantage. This is why globalization is powerful as a driver of global consumption between countries of all capabilities.

One of the major potential benefits of globalization is to provide opportunities for reducing macroeconomic volatility on output and consumption via diversification of risk. The overall evidence of the globalization effect on macroeconomic volatility of output indicates that although direct effects are ambiguous in theoretical models, financial integration helps in a nation's production base diversification, and leads to an increase in specialization of production. However, the specialization of production, based on the concept of comparative advantage, can also lead to higher volatility in specific industries within an economy and society of a nation. As time passes, successful companies, independent of size, will be the ones that are part of the global economy.

Empirical evidence suggests that a positive growth effect takes place in countries that are sufficiently rich when it comes to globalization. For investors and economies, globalization also provides the opportunity to reduce the volatility of output and consumption, since products and services can be imported or exported with greater ease. Fewer "bubbles" arise from a mismatch in supply and demand if the production of goods and services is more elastic. But, when all countries can develop to become developed countries, globalization developed countries which may also bring these disadvantages as below:

Drawbacks of globalization

Globalization is often criticized for taking away jobs from domestic companies and workers. After all, the U.S. cement industry will go out of business if imports from a developing country drive down prices, even if consumption increases. Small U.S. cement companies would find it difficult to compete and likely shut down, leaving workers unemployed, while the larger U.S. cement industry would likely experience a significant protracted decline.

A second criticism is the high cost of a comparative or absolute advantage to a country's own well-being if mismanaged. For example, China has become a leading worldwide emitter of carbon dioxide thanks to its comparative advantage in manufacturing a wide range of products. Other countries may have a comparative advantage in mining certain natural resources—such as crude oil—and mishandle the revenue generated from those activities.

A final disadvantage of globalization is the increase in wages for workers, which can hurt corporate profitability. For example, if a rich country has a high comparative advantage in developing software, they may drive up the price of software engineers around the world, which makes it difficult for foreign companies to compete in the market.

The phenomenon of globalization began in a primitive form when humans first settled into different areas of the world; however, it has shown a rather steady and rapid progress in recent times and has become an international dynamic which, due to technological advancements, has increased in speed and scale, so that countries in all five continents have been affected and engaged.

What Is Globalization? Why and how globalization may achieve when global countries can develop to become developed countries ?

Globalization is defined as a process that, based on international strategies, aims to expand business operations on a worldwide level, and was precipitated by the facilitation of global communications due to technological advancements, and socioeconomic, political and environmental developments.

The goal of globalization is to provide organizations a superior competitive position with lower operating costs, to gain greater numbers of products, services, and consumers. This approach to competition is gained via diversification of resources, the creation and development of new investment opportunities by opening up additional markets and accessing new raw materials and resources. Diversification of resources is a business strategy that increases the variety of business products and services within various organizations. Diversification strengthens institutions by lowering organizational risk factors, spreading interests in different areas, taking advantage of market opportunities, and acquiring companies both horizontal and vertical in nature.

Industrialized or developed nations are specific countries with a high level of economic development and meet certain socioeconomic criteria based on economic theory, such as gross domestic product (GDP), industrialization and human development index (HDI) as defined by the International Monetary Fund (IMF), the United Nations (UN) and the World Trade Organization (WTO). Using these definitions, some industrialized countries are: United Kingdom, Belgium, Denmark, Finland, France, Germany, Japan, Luxembourg, Norway, Sweden, Switzerland, and the United States.

Components of Globalization

The components of globalization include GDP, industrialization and the Human Development Index (HDI). The GDP is the market value of all finished goods and services produced within a country's borders in a year and serves as a measure of a country's overall economic output. Industrialization is a process which, driven by technological innovation, effectuates social change and economic development by transforming a country into a modernized industrial, or developed nation. The Human Development Index comprises three components: a country's population's life expectancy, knowledge and education measured by the adult literacy, and income.

The degree to which an organization is globalized and diversified has bearing on the strategies that it uses to pursue greater development and investment opportunities.

When all countries can become developed countries. They may bring the Economic Impact on Developed Nations as below: Globalization compels businesses to adapt to different strategies based on new ideological trends that try to balance the rights and interests of both the individual and the community as a whole. This change enables businesses to compete worldwide and also signifies a dramatic change for business leaders, labor and management by legitimately accepting the participation of workers and government in developing and implementing company policies and strategies. Risk reduction via diversification can be accomplished through company involvement with international financial institutions and partnering with both local and multinational businesses.

Globalization brings reorganization at the international, national and sub-national levels. Specifically, it brings the reorganization of production, international trade and the integration of financial markets. This affects capitalist economic and social relations, via multilateralism and microeconomic phenomena, such as business competitiveness, at the global level. The transformation of production systems affects the class structure, the labor process, the application of technology and the structure and organization of capital. Globalization is now seen as marginalizing the less educated and low-skilled workers. Business expansion will no longer automatically imply increased employment. Additionally, it can cause a high remuneration of capital, due to its higher mobility compared to labor.

The phenomenon seems to be driven by three major forces: the globalization of all product and financial markets, technology, and deregulation. Globalization of product and financial markets refers to an increased economic integration in specialization and economies of scale, which will result in greater trade in financial services through both capital flows and cross-border entry activity. The technology factor, specifically telecommunication and information availability, has facilitated remote delivery and provided new access and distribution channels, while revamping industrial structures for financial services by allowing entry of non-bank entities, such as telecoms and utilities.

When all countries can become developed countries. In a global economic view, power is the ability of a company to command both tangible and intangible assets that create customer loyalty, regardless of location. Independent of size or geographic location, a company can meet global standards and tap into global networks, thrive and act as a world-class thinker, maker, and trader, by using its greatest assets: its concepts, competence, and connections. When all developing countries become developed countries, they may bring these beneficial effects as below:

Some economists have a positive outlook regarding the net effects of globalization on economic growth. These effects have been analyzed over the years by several studies attempting to measure the impact of globalization on various nations' economies using variables such as trade, capital flows, and their openness, GDP per capita, foreign direct investment (FDI) and more. These studies examined the effects of several components of globalization on growth using time-series cross-sectional data on trade, FDI and portfolio investment. Although they provide an analysis of individual components of globalization on economic growth, some of the results are inconclusive or even contradictory. However, overall, the findings of those studies seem to be supportive of the economists' positive position, instead of the one held by the public and non-economist view.

Trade among nations via the use of comparative advantage promotes growth, which is attributed to a strong correlation between the openness to trade flows and the effect on economic growth and economic performance. Additionally, there is a strong positive relation between capital flows and their impact on economic growth. Foreign Direct Investment's impact on economic growth has had a positive growth effect in wealthy countries and an increase in trade and FDI, resulting in higher growth rates.8 Empirical research examining the effects of several components of globalization on growth, using time series and cross-sectional data on trade, FDI and portfolio investment, found that a country tends to have a lower degree of globalization if it generates higher revenues from trade taxes. Further evidence indicates that there is a positive growth-effect in countries that are sufficiently rich, as are most of the developed nations.

The World Bank reports that integration with global capital markets can lead to disastrous effects, without sound domestic financial systems. One of the potential benefits of globalization is to provide opportunities for reducing macroeconomic volatility on output and consumption via diversification of risk.

However, when all countries can become developed countries, they may also bring these harmful effects as below:

Non-economists and the wide public expect the costs associated with globalization to outweigh the benefits, especially in the short-run. Less wealthy countries from those among the industrialized nations may not have the same highly-accentuated beneficial effect from globalization as more wealthy countries, measured by GDP per capita, etc. Although free trade increases opportunities for international trade, it also increases the risk of failure for smaller companies that cannot compete globally.

Additionally, free trade may drive up production and labor costs, including higher wages for a more skilled workforce, which again can lead to outsourcing jobs from countries with higher wages. Moreover, domestic industries in some countries may be endangered due to comparative or absolute advantage of other countries in specific industries. Another possible danger and harmful effect is the overuse and abuse of natural resources to meet new higher demands in the production of goods.

In overall, when all countries can develop to become developed countries, they may bring these general benefits to influence our society to bring positive changes. They may include: Globalization activity doesn't only reduce trade boundary but it lot more effects like one country come closer to the economy of other country, it help in mixture of culture, it helps in transfer information and technology, increase group of buyer and seller of products and services etc. this are only few advantages of globalizations. Due to globalization trade is getting more interdependent and to protect interest of every nation W.T.O keep a close look over the trade of every nation. Due globalization many environmental threats are evolved every country is moving toward industrialization which increase global warming and it is needed to be checked. Social problem are also occurred like exploitation of labour, increase in child labour in developing nations, lack of powerful labour union etc this social problem are needed to taken care of and proper law should be made to avoid such kind of problems. As every things as has some advantages, it also has some disadvantages also.

Advantages:
- New market for product.
- Helps in growth of economy.
- Increase in infrastructure.
- Free flow of technology and information.
- Reduction in poverty.
- Increases in employments.
- International body governs trade through its law, so interest of every country should be protected.

Disadvantages are as follows:
- It brings competitions because of which small scale industries suffer in under develop countries.
- Globalization lead to growth in infrastructure but on other hand it bring harm to environment due to industrialization, reduction in forest areas.

● Due to globalization environment, labour, resource of under develop countries are exploited by develop countries.
● Poor trade union.
● Lack of control over country economy by its governments.

Effect of globalization on developing countries or third world countries

The thinking of first world, second world and third world countries are given by U.S.A which place itself as the first world nation, European countries as second world nations and as far as third world country are concerned under develop and developing countries come under this categories. The third world countries are further classified as under developed countries and developing countries. In under developed, countries like Afghanistan, Nepal, Bangladesh, Nigeria, Bhutan, Pakistan etc comes this are the growing nations but as far as development of economy is concerned they are far behind. In developing countries, countries like China, India, South Africa, Brazil etc are included because this are among fastest growing nation after globalization has taken place. But under develop countries are not much benefited because of this globalization process. Rather than getting benefit they are exploited. In a sense, due to cheap labour these countries manpower is exploited and it natural resource is been taken away as we can take the example of china, china is investing a lot in African nation and on exchange of this it is utilizing its natural resources.

What influences to the countries like china and India has grown tremendously after globalization.

Before globalizations export of china was not very high but now it is one the global leader in exports and as far as India is concerned before India was accounted only for 0.6 % of world export and now it is accounted for 1 % of world exports. Brazil has also show huge growth its per capita income has also increased. Countries like Bhutan, Malaysia, Indonesia etc has tremendous growth in GDP in past five years. Outsourcing has increased in these nations. Now India earns 51% of GDP from service sectors and its service sector is growing tremendously because of it excellence in IT sectors and this boosted up after globalizations. Now china earns major part of it GDP from export which increased after globalization. As far as Latin America is concerned Brazil has show tremendous growth in export, technology and manufacturing sectors. And now it is among top five of developing nations.

Effect of globalization on developed countries when all developing countries can become developed countries

Due to globalization the develop countries are moving towards underdeveloped countries like India, China, Indonesia etc for outsourcing their job to these countries because of cheap labour. Nowadays develop nation are coming to under develop nation for setting up manufacturing plants in these nation because of its availability of cheap and skilled labours. Due to globalization develop countries are facing intense competition from underdeveloped countries, competition in sense employment, exports, technology etc. Due to globalization developed countries are also exploit resources like natural resource, manpower, and environment etc. of underdeveloped nations. Also, due to globalization the dominance of developed nation is also reducing. The people of developed nation are facing intense competition for job from people growing nation like china, India, Thailand etc. now for FDI in developed nation are reducing due increase in the FDI in developing countries like china, Brazil, India etc. Thus, when all developing countries can develop to become developed countries in future one day. Globalization developed countries got new market for their products and services, and new place for their business expansions.

Development of "Regional economic" will truly help India to build viable economic future for its citizens.

Due to globalization various effect and development has take place which help india to build viable economic future for its citizens. Due Globalization to this the infrastructure of India has developed a lot because of which transportation, sanitary, hygiene, sports complex and stadium has developed a lot and still developing which will give better environment for future generation. Nowadays, foreign education institutes are coming to india which has increased the level of education. Export of india is increasing with each quarter which help to reduce the fiscal deficit and increase the GDP of the nation.

Nowadays more and more manufacturing industries are established because of which more employment is created and hence improving per capita income of the nation. Due globalization India is more concerned about the global warming and planning its growth in such a way that it could reduce it contribution in global. And it will be helpful for future citizens.

Regional economies help to reduce domination of developed economies on the developing economies.

Developments in regional economy will strength the self reliability of the nation which will help to reduction in the dependence on other nation. Development of regional economy will lead to increase in GDP, Standard of living, Per capita income of the nation. If India wants to emerge as supper power it has to develop it regional because it is the stepping stone toward it. In conclusion, when all countries can develop to achieve developed countries. They will create development of regional economy to our global societies. Then, they may bring these benefits in possible. They may include: Development of regional economy will lead to reduce in inequalities of distribution of wealth, development of regional economy will lead to increase in metropolitan culture, development of regional economy will lead increase the contributions of every state in Indian GDP, development of regional economy will lead to reduction of poverty, unemployment and illiteracy.

2. Economic growth advantages and disadvantages

When all developing countries can develop to be developed countries, then it may also bring global economic growth. However, I believe that when global societies can have sudden economic growth in short time, due to all or many developing countries can develop to be developed countries in success. They may bring advantages and disadvantages both aspects as below:

Economic development can be describe as the development of economic wealth of countries or regions for the well-being of their inhabitants such as the improvement and innovation on the political, economic, and social of its people. Economic development and growth are totally different in terms which are used in economics. Economic development refers to economic growth which accompanied by changes in economic structure and output distribution. So, economic growth may be necessary but not sufficient to attain economic development. Thus, peoples always said that economic development is the problems of underdeveloped countries and economic growth to those of developed countries. Underdeveloped countries always face some problems such as low income, weakness of human resource and also the economic vulnerability. These problems also made the countries hard to attain the development of economic. However, for those developed countries, they do not face the same problems as what underdeveloped countries do, therefore, they are more easily to attain the economic development and treat it as an economic growth.

In addition, in the term of economic development is much more comprehensive because it implies progressive changes in the socio-economic structure of a country. Nowadays, the evolution of new technology is directly related to economic development. Without high technology in a country, it is hard to bring an economic development toward its people. Viewed in this way economic development involves a steady decline in agricultural shares in GNP and continuous increase in shares of industries, trade banking construction and services. However, economic growth just only refers to the rise in total output in a country; development implies change in technological and institutional organization of production as well as in distributive pattern of income. Hence, if compared to the goal of development, economic growth is much easy to realize. Between, we just need a larger mobilization of resources and raising their productivity by enhance it to be more efficiency and effective, then the output level can be raised and economic growth will occur. However, the development process is far more extensive than the economic growth. Not only a rise in output, it also involved changes in composition of output, and shift in the allocation of productive resources, and reduction or elimination of poverty, inequalities and unemployment. However, economic development is impossible without having an economic growth but economic growth is possible without an economic development. Growth is just increase in GNP but it does not have any other parameters to it; unlike development which can be conceived as Multi-Dimensional process.

Are economic growth and development worthwhile?
Economic growth and development have their advantages and also disadvantages. Although economic growth widens the range of human choices, but this may not necessarily bring happiness toward people. Happiness is dependent on the relationship between wants and resources. People may become more satisfied, not only by having more wants met, but perhaps also by renouncing certain material goods. Wealth may make people less happy if it increases wants more than resources. Furthermore, acquisitive and achievement-oriented societies may be more likely to give rise to individual frustration.

Advantages
Economic growth will decreases famine, starvation, infant mortality, and death; gives us greater leisure; can enhance art, music, and philosophy; and gives us the resources to be humanitarian. Economic growth will especially benefit to societies in which political desire exceed the resources, because it may prevent what might otherwise prove to be social tension that people

can't take it. However, without economic growth, the desires of one group can be met when others expense on it. Lastly, economic growth can help newly independent countries in mobilizing resources to increase the power of a nation.

Disadvantages

Growth has its value. First, the disadvantage might be the acquisitiveness, materialism, and dissatisfaction with one's present state associated with a society's economic struggles. Second, liquidity, objective, and self-associated with economic growth may undermine the reliance on extended family system, in fact, the focus of the prevailing social structure. Third, economic growth, which depends on the rational and technological innovation and changes in scientific methods, often is the threat in religious and social authority. Fourth, economic growth often require more specialized work, which may be caused by more objective, accompanied more drab and monotonous tasks, more discipline, and a pair of process loss.

In addition, economic growth which follow by large organizational units are more likely to lead to bureaucratization, objective, communication problems, and the use of force were consistent. Economic growth and development of large enterprises with a manufacturer's products and services while demand increased, and urban growth, this may be is accompanied byrootlessness, environmental blight disease, and unhealthy living conditions, even in the narrow social values change and may ultimately lead to a new dynamic equilibrium that is better than the old static equilibrium, the transition could have some very painful issues. In addition, the political transformation, as rapid economic growth, may lead to greater concentration, stress, social disruption, even authoritarian. Therefore, even if the population seriously committed to economic growth, its implementation is not likely at all costs pursued. All societies must take into account that the conflicts with the maximization of economic growth and other objectives. Because it was want sits in high level positions, a developing country own citizens can promote the local production control to reduce the growth in the short term.

The question now is what will be weighed to achieve an orderly, stable society, and maintain traditional values and culture, and promoting political autonomy? Economic growth is the increase a country's per capita output. Economic development, economic growth has resulted in the poorest strata of the population or level of education, changes to improve the output distribution of economic welfare and economic changes in different structures.

Economic growth and development of Asia when all or many developing countries can develop to be developed countries

Nowadays, economic development in Asia shows high impact of economic development of this respective continent. Economy of Asia has taken an important part in the view of the world's economy. These continents have adopted one of the following economic systems such as capitalism, socialism, communism, and fascism. As we know, Asia is the largest continent in terms of area surface and also the population. Beside it, it is also the region with the highest growth rate. Below are Asian countries that contribute their economic development to our society.

Of all the Asian Countries, the only Asian country included among the industrialized countries is Japan. According to the International Monetary Fund, the country per capita was GDP 32,608 U.S. dollars or in 2009, the 23rd highest on record. Moreover, according to certain criteria, the term means that developed countries is the countries that having a high level of development. What standards and which countries are classified as being developed, is a controversial issue which surrounded by a fierce debate. Thus, economic criteria tend to dominate discussions. Countries which having per capita income and high per capita gross domestic product (GDP) will be described as developed countries. Another criterion is the industrialization; countries in the tertiary and quaternary sector-of industry leading will be described as development. Another recent measure, the human development index, which combines economic measures, and other measures of national income, life expectancy and education indicators, have become prominent. This criterion will define the development country as those very high (HDI) rating. However, many exceptions exist when the decision to "developed country" status is used to measure the subject. Countries do not fit this definition are classified as developing countries.

However, Taiwan, Hong Kong and Singapore are regarded as newly industrialized countries. The category of newly industrialized country (NIC) is a socioeconomic classification which applied to various countries in the world by political scientists and economists. NIC is the nation's economy has not yet reached first world status, but in the macro sense, the development of the countries is normally faster than counterpart. Another feature of newly industrialized countries is that undergoing in rapid economic growth (usually export-oriented). However, the starting or ongoing industrialization is an important indicator of NIC. In many newly industrialized countries, may also be experiencing social unrest by major primary rural, or agricultural, populations migrate to the cities, where the thousand of laborers can be draw by growth of manufacturing concerns and factories. In the social development process, it usually shares some characteristic such as increased social freedoms and civil rights, strong political leadership, which switch from an agricultural to an industrial economy, the other common features, especially in the manufacturing sector, an increasingly open market economy with free trade and other heavy capital investment from countries around the world. In addition, the political leadership in their area of influence and lastly is they have lowered poverty rates.

I shall indicate China, Philippines, India, North Korea these developing country when they can become developed country , what it can bring global social change influence example. Moreover, as we know, the history and culture of China is their secret to improve their economy, even if it ruled and control by their state. Prior to 1979, China maintained a centrally planned or command economy. The economy of China with the large proportion is directed by the state which established production goals, controlled prices, distribution, and most of the economic control of resources. During the 1950s, all of China's individual household farms were collectivized into large communes. To support rapid industrialization, the central government starts to take large-scale physical and human capital investment during 1960-1970s. As a result, by 1978, nearly three quarters of industrial production generated by the central control of state-owned enterprises according to centrally planned output targets. Private enterprises and foreign invested enterprises are almost non-existent.

A central objective of Chinese government was to make China's economy relatively self-sufficient. Foreign trade was generally limited to those commodity which unable to obtain or receive the goods in China. The Government's policy to keep the Chinese economy relatively stagnant and inefficient, mainly because of where the profits of some enterprises and farmers to stimulate competition, in fact, does not exist, price and production controls caused widespread economic distortions. China's standard of living is much lower than those of many other.

In addition, India is contributing in business process outsourcing improvement for the information technology which has a significant impact for the economic development in South Asia. The Philippines is improving, because they help to remittances from abroad, they send money to their loved ones from overseas Filipino workers to improve their country. North Korea shows hammer and sling as a symbol for their communistic views of their economic system in Far East Asia. While South Korea shows modern technology that is influence from Western countries which results an improvement of technology in their designated countries. Indonesia is a Muslim country, the whole of Asia's largest population by the Dutch colony. It is based on their banking and finance in the Islamic way of life. This is also the case in Malaysia was a British colony.

After analyze the information of some Asian Countries, I discovered that they are facing several problems in economic development. First, they have low standard of living, low level of production, there is a rapid population growth, they having a high rate of unemployment, lastly, there are over dependence on agricultural production and exportation of raw materials and also the international trade.

Economic growth and development of Malaysia

According to the recent The Star's newspaper, Malaysia economic development is one of fastest and steady in global economic scenario. Malaysia GDP per capita has been estimated to be $15,700 in fiscal year 2008. This is a clear indication of tremendous economic development in Malaysia. Malaysia economy is a middle income country that has developed since 1970's. It was previously a mere raw materials producing economy, which has evolved now as a developing multi-sector economy. This growth bears testimony to impressive economic development at Malaysia. Prime Minister Abdullah, after coming to power in 2003, has tried to develop economy of this south Asian country by introducing value added production. He took a number of measures to introduce hi-tech technologies and encouraged investments in high technology industries, medical technology and pharmaceuticals. Efforts have been made by government of Malaysia to stop its dependence on export products. However, exports of electronics goods have always been a major factor in Malaysia economy. There has been huge profit accrued from export of oil and gas and it has been a major factor for Malaysia economic development. There have been huge profits from high energy prices, although there was high cost of gasoline and diesel fuel. This, however, made Kuala Lumpur minimize financial assistance of government. It has been found that currency value of Malaysia has hiked 6 percent per year when pitted against dollar in fiscal years 2006 to 2008.

Model of economy development: The production function how can be influenced to change when many or all developing countries can become developed countries

In macroeconomics, the production function is a function which specifies combination of all input from the output. In the macro-economy, production functions are functions that determine the output of a company which entered all combinations of input. A meta-production function comparing the practices of companies that has to change input to output to determine the function of the most efficient production practices of the entity that is, whether the most efficient production practices that qualify or production practices that are actually the most efficient. In these cases, the maximum output production process technology is defined as mathematical function of one or more entered. In other words, given a collection of all technical combination allows the output and input, just include a combination of maximum output for a given set of inputs to the production or function. Production function can be defined as specification of minimum input requirements needed to produce a total output that was, by given current technology. It is usually assumed that the production of unique functions can be built for every production technology.

Assuming when many or all developing countries can develop to become developed countries in future one day, they may bring these influences to our social technologic production function changes as below:

The maximum output possible from the set of technology inputs of all, the economic use in the production function analysis is the abstract essence of the technical and managerial problems associated with a specific production process. Engineering and managerial problems of technical competence is assumed to be broken, so the analysis can focus on the problem of efficiency allocate. States are assumed to make choices about how much each input of allocate factors put to use and how much output to produce, remember the cost (purchase price) of each factor, the sale price of output, and the factors represent technology to determine its production function. Frame results in one or more constant input can be used, for example, capital can be assumed to be fixed (constant) in the short term, and labor and possibly other variables such as input raw material, while in the long run, the quantity of capital and the factors that can be made by the company are variable. In the long term, companies may even have the choice of technology, represented by the various functions of production as possible.

Input to output relationship is non-financial, that the production function relating physical inputs to physical outputs, and prices and the cost is reflected in the function. But the production function is not a complete model of the production process: intentionally abstract from the inherent aspects of physical production process that some would consider extremely important, including error, entropy or waste. In addition, the production functions do not typically model business processes, well, ignoring the role of management. (For primer on the basic elements of the production of Microeconomics theory, see production theory policies).

The main purpose of the production function is to address allocate efficiency in the use of input factors in production and distribution of factory income such factors. Based on certain assumptions, the production function can be used to reduce a marginalized product for each factor, which implies an ideal division of the revenue generated from the output to the income from their every input factor of production.

How global developed economy influences household expenditure decision?

In the saving function, there is a mathematical relation between saving and income by the household sector. Thus, the saving function can be stated as an equation such as a simple linear equation or a diagram indicated as the saving line. This function captures the relationship between savings and income, one of the other sides the relationship between consumer incomes, constitutes a cornerstone of Keynesian economics. The two key function to save the parameters are intercept, which indicates that self-saving, side slope, which is the marginal propensity to save, show that the induced savings. The injection- leakage model used in Keynesian economics is based on the saving function.

Saving function on Keynesian economics is the starting point for determination of equilibrium output injection, leakage model. It captures the household sector in which the relationship between savings and income. As the income for either consumption or savings to use, saving feature is the complementary consumption function. Reflects the fundamental psychological law put forward by John Maynard Keynes, consumer spending (and saving by the household sector) depends on the income and just some of the revenue is used for consumption and saving the rest. This function is presented either as a mathematical formula, usually as a simple linear equation, graph or savings line. In either form, income is a measure of disposable income, national income and GDP. However, the saving function makes it easy to divide saving into two basic types such as the autonomous saving and Induced saving. Autonomous saving is the intercept term. Induced saving is the slope. Lastly, the slope of marginal propensity to save (MPS) also considered as saving function

How global developed economy influences the labor supply function changes ?

In mainstream economic theory, labor supply is the total number of hours number of a workers want to work in a given real wage rate. From the diagram above, we can see the positive relationship between the wages rate and also the quantity of labor. When the wage rate is low, the quantity of the labor also is low. However, when there is a rose in wage rate will also increase the quantity of labor. Realistically, the labor supply is the role of various factors within an economy. For example, as a heavy increased of population will make downward pressure on wages which may lead to high unemployment.

How global developed economy influences wage rate versus labor leisure changes?

Labor supply curves are derived from the 'labor-leisure' trade-off. More hours worked earn higher incomes but necessitate a cut in the amount of leisure that workers enjoy. Therefore, there are two aspects, to provide the necessary amount of labor is due to changes in real wage rates. For example, the real wage rate raises the opportunity cost of leisure increases as the diagram shows above. This tends to cause workers to supply more labor (the "substitution effect"). However, as the real wage rate rises, workers earn a higher income for a given number of hours. If leisure is a normal good – the demand for it increases as income increases – this increase in income will tend to cause workers to supply less labor (the "income effect"). If the "substitution effect" is stronger than the "income effect" then the labor supply curve will be upward sloping and vice versa.

However, from the view of Marxist, a labor supply is a core requirement in a capitalist society. In order to avoid Labor shortage and ensure a labor supply, a large portion of the population must not possess sources of self-provisioning, which would allow them to be independent, and they must instead be compelled, in order to survive, to sell their labor for a subsistence wage.

Economic development theories: Harrod-Domar theory
When all or many countries can develop to be developed countries, how they can influence global technological growth rate changes. The Harrod-Domar theory delineates a functional economic relationship in which the growth rate of gross domestic product (g) depends directly on the national saving ratio (s) and inversely on the national capital/output ratio (k) so that it is written a $g = s / k$. The equation takes its name from a synthesis of analyses of growth process by two economists (Sir Roy Harrod of Britain and E.V. Domar of the USA). The Harrod-Domar model in the early postwar times was commonly used by developing countries in economic planning. With a target growth rate, the required saving rate is known. If the country is not capable of generating that level of saving, a justification or an excuse for borrowing from international agencies can be established. An example in the Asian context is to ascertain the relationship between high growth rates and high saving rates in the cases of Japan and China. It is more difficult to introduce the third building block of a growth model, the labor and population element. In the long run, growth rate is constrained by population growth and also by the rate of technological change.

● Climate change will impact developed countries to continue develop

Will developed countries become
developing countries
● Why does illness can cause global economic recession to developed countries

Firstly, I shall explain why unpredicted illness factor can cause developed countries' economic recession. Although developed countries have advantages and let people to believe that their any medical, economic, education, business etc. different industries aspects are developed in mature. Their these any industries aspects are better or are improved better to compare the developing countries. But, in fact, whether it is possible that their any industries aspects will become worse to compare developing countries when they do not continue to improve any one of their industries aspects. I shall indiate whether what factors my cause developed countries to become developing countries in possible.
Many developing countries are facing problem very different from that of the developed countries. Countries such as Japan, Germany are facing depleting population whether on the other side countries like India,

Indonesia are facing severe resource crunch due to population explosion. In such situation measuring the progress of the countries on the same scales decided by developed industrialized world is injustice to these countries. Developed world have achieved there parameters after journey of around 200-250 years post industrialization while many developing countries are in their 60s-70s after getting freedom from crutches of colonialism. In such cases developing countries should formulate their own parameters for growth and development and continue their progress. So, it seems that any developing countries will have possible to develop to be better any developed countries. Otherwise, any developed countries will have possible to bring worse development when they have many people loss jobs. For example, US economy will go down nowadays, due to the Chinese serious illness influences many US people die. Many US businessmen can not continue to manufacture or sell their products because many people can not go to offices or factories to work. They need to stay at homes to avoid the illness attacks when they need to contact the illness people in workplace, or they are walking on streets, or they are catching any public transport. So,although US is one developed country, but it can not still to avoid this China illness attack. It is possible due to US government neglects to consider this China illness is one kind of death sick to cause US has many people to die easily in this year 2020. If US government can prohibit to let Chinese travellers to enter its country when China has occurred this serious illness caused in 2019 last year. These Chiness illness people can not enter US to cause this kind of illness to attack any US people lung to cause they die. After it is possible that US can avoid to cause many US people to die. So, it does not consider whether the country is developed or not to avoid global economic recession, because it is illness factor to cause developed countries' economic recession, such as US, UK nowadays economic recession.

● Increasing social crime rate and government assistance may cause developed countries to become developing coutries

Secondly, I shall explain why increasing social crime rate or many young people do criminal behaviors in society, it can influence developed countries to develop worse or can not develop better in its society. Otherwise, when on developing countries have less crime rate or decreases its crime rate, it can develop better or improve its society to be better. For a developing country to catch up to a developed country, it must not only grow, but grow faster than the developed country. While It is possible for such accelerated growth to occur through rapid industrialization, but there are many country-specific factors that directly affect a developing country's ability to catch up to developed countries. They range from growth of productivity, labour force participation rate, standard of living, infrastructure, political environment etc.

For example, when the developing country can improve its education quality to let many young people learn any kinds of new knowledge to like do any kinds of jobs, even, driving , factory labor, waiters, etc. low educational level jobs in society. Then, it will reduce its crime rate when many young people feel need to work. They won't need government to assist their life. Consequently, it will have possible to develop its economy or improve its economy to be better. In education primarily is the most essential quality that helps to empower the people of the country to communicate and achieve a common objective and is thus an extremely important driver for the developing to developed country journey. This is a common observation in all the developing countries. The one area that is still a struggle is education. Also, lack of education leads to increased poverty and disparity of income which leads to the 2nd most hindrance in a countries journey to achieve a developed nation status. Maybe if the path chosen is that of streamlining lack of education, poverty, a more driven and focused effort with individuals who know and can fathom the importance of this change working towards achieving a developed nation status can be undertaken. A semi-industrial, pro-human development approach should be a path adopted to see a qualitative shift in reducing this gap.

All through our education we have learnt 'India is a developing country' which brings to thought, will it ever be recognized as a 'developed country'? And what is the criteria to qualify as a developed nation? Are these criteria set by the developed nations to meet their convenience? If this is the case it would be more logical for developing nations to set their own criteria. It gets very difficult for developing nations to meet the criteria set by the giant economies, as even a single step gone wrong could ruin the effort of years. India can be seen as an example, where the step of demonetization and GST together led to a growth rate of 5.7%, weakest growth rate since the first quarter of 2014. These steps would probably have a positive effect in the long run and it is worth the wait. Another question to bring our attention to is, are the developed countries developed in the true sense? Considering the parameter of crime rate, USA has a very high crime rate. Another aspect could be unemployment, again US has a good percent of unemployed individuals every year. So, aren't the developed nations also falling short? It may be a good strategy for developing nations could be establishing a path which would help them use their resources aptly and generate output for their people.

In this race of matching with the developed nations we are leading nowhere, better we set a different goal all together. Every nation has a different potential given different kinds of resources they possess hence expecting the same output from all makes little sense. Hope the coming generation gets to learn, 'India is a developed country in the true sense'. Hence, high crime rate, such as US has high crime rate. Because it has many young people do not like to work, they depend on government assistance. Then, any kinds of low skill or low educational level job employers will feel difficult to find them to work. Then, their society will cause low skillful labour shortage challange. It is not due to US lacks enough low skill or low educational workers, it is due to they do not like to work, they feel wages are less , when their government can give any money or loss job allowance to support their lives in long time. It can enough these low educational level or low skillful level young people choose not work. Then, this US developed country will not have any young people to do any service job, e.g. driving public transport, waiter, security. When these kinds of job old people need to retire, these employers can not find any young people to replace them to do these service jobs. They can only choose to employ another old age people to replace the retired service staffs. Then, these kinds any one of service jobs can not raise their service level, their service performance will be worse or keep the same service level, it means that their performance can not perform better level to serve their clients in US society. It implies that developed country, such as US its general social service level will be worse or they can not be improved to satisfy their client needs. In this developed country's poor service environment, how to explain it can still keep its developed country's position , such as US.

However, it may bring the question -Will Developing Countries ever catch up with Developed Countries? will remain unanswered because you have rightly pointed out that leaders of developing countries have given up on the economy and they keep themselves busy with other matters. Political institutions has great impact on the development of a nation. Industrial revolution happened in England instead of any other country because England had the best political institution that time. We have been hearing that if the 20th century belonged to developed countries of North America and Europe then 21st century will be of developing countries such as India,

China and Brazil. But development is the crucial word which draws boundary between two countries-developed or developing. According to the World Bank reducing poverty is the main purpose of the development. After the World War 2, many nations have had significant growth however only few have been able to catch up with developed countries in terms of per capita income. From 1940s till 1990s poor countries grew slowly, falling farther behind to rich ones in income. Only few countries such as South Korea and Singapore were able to gain rich status. Since 2000, developing nations such as India and China are economically growing and managing growth rates of above 10% per year. With such continuous growth rates, developing nations can converge with developed nations and that would mean higher standard of living and good economic and political power. But this growth is limited to few countries since many countries still have not opened their domestic market to international markets. These countries also have barriers in technology and availability and allocation of resources. So, it seems that developing countries still need more time to develop exceed to the developed countries because they, such as China, Korea, Taiwan , Singapore etc. have poor technology and shortage of allocation or resource to compare the developed countries, such as US, UK etc. even their crime rate may reduce or many young people may accept to do the low skillful or low education level service jobs in societies.

● Developed countries lack effort to manufacture cheap products to sell strengths

Hence, we need to look at every economy as a company and developing a unique selling proposition becomes relevant. The United States has a USP of being the most technologically advanced and productive country. China has managed to become an exporter of cheap goods, the United Kingdom till now was a financial hub- there are chances of that changing thanks to BREXIT with the rise of Dublin. When we look at developing economies, such as India, we do not see any USP in the making. What is India's USP? I cannot think of any. People talk about demographic dividend to India in terms of a large young population. Such a population, which is largely uneducated is a demographic curse. Merely being a large market for goods and services is a bad idea for a USP. Developing countries need to introspect sometimes to look at the systemic challenges that they face. Looking towards developed economies is not always the best alternative. Such as China can choose to buy cheap product, because its technologic developement is poor. It is its strength to manufacture cheap products to sell to overseas to earn foreign income and raise GDP on export aspect. So, China may have much development chance to grow up its economy when it can decide which kinds of cheap or easier manufacturing products to sell to overseas when these countries can not supply from themselves manufactures, they need to buy from China in long time.

While the share of many western economies remained very low. However, over the years the trend started to reverse and many western countries have now become very developed while third world countries like India, China etc. continue on their journey from being developing to developed. We are currently a 2 trillion dollar economy and the eighth largest economy in the world. By 2030, India is predicted to be the fifth largest economy in the world. On purchasing power basis, India is the second largest economy in the world only behind China. Despite so many bright spots, we are faced with the paradox of being an advanced economy and still being one of the poorest in the world.

Otherwise, many such countries who are highly rich in natural resources continue to be plundered by the developed economies. Many countries continue to be haunted by the choices they made in past and turnaround being highly unlikely. They are often not helped by the injustices meted out by the developed economies who continue to take decision in their own self-interest. I feel the time has come when all the developing economies need to unite and raise their voice collectively. They need to speak about the unfair treatment meted out to them. A step in this regard has been taken by countries like India and China in important forums like UN and WTO. These breakout countries can act like role models and help create a more equitable world.

Another country is India, developing country , it may choose to manufacture and sell cheap products to any overeas countries to earn high GDP trade income. Till about 1750s, India was one of the largest economies in the world, contributing close to 25% of the world GDP. It was called the 'Golden Bird' and its products were world famed. The country has had huge trade surpluses for centuries through export of spices, finished cloth ('light woven air', it was called), and diamonds; all exotic products to that time period. It also had a thriving shipbuilding industry. There were accounts of Roman Establishments worrying about their riches syphoning off to India, because of the love of their woman towards Indian Cloth. India, thus essentially provided what the world desired & craved for, taking very few in return. This is despite the fact that it had one of the largest populations of that time. Then how come Indians achieve that richness and advancement, which seems difficult now? It is because, India was a hotbed of skilled people, who created exotic products, which were taken to the world by merchants in Indian built ships, which in turn were financed adequately by an established network of local people. So, although, India is not one high technologic development country, but it can choose what kinds of general cheap products to manufacture or catch any natural resources, e.g. growing up fishing industry, diamond industry. It is any one developed countries can not own strengths to compete to India easily.

Modern India and the ilk, are that they should spend more on Education and encourage Individual/SMEs (Small and Medium scale Enterprises), through adequate financing. The educational infrastructure should go to every nook and corner of the country like the 'temple complexes' providing accessible and affordable education, in the form of 'community colleges' in the US & 'skill enhancement centres'. Governments should support with adequate funds to create world-class universities of yesterday like 'The Nalanda', to provide cross-functional education and focus on innovation. The population should be encouraged to innovate & produce products, the world desires, like the 'light muslin cloth' or the 'iPhone' of the modern day, which shall bring huge trade surpluses. Industrialization should be decentralized through support for SMEs rather than purely going for High scale Industries. The financial infrastructure should be expanded enough to provide the financial support to every citizen, through banking services. Thus, on the whole, history can provide us with a lot of lessons on how to go about things, provided we have the interest to see from where we have come from. These lessons can be modified and applied to the current times, for we know these lands have done it before, for centuries. But, the only thing that requires here is 'Conviction' and if every country starts working on building these capacities, they becoming developed economies is just a matter of time!

● Climate change will impact developed countries to continue develop

Why does climate change impact developed countries to continue develop more easily? It is one natural environment hurt problem , due to human,e.g. businessmen their damage our global natural environment behaviors, to cause any one developed countries may become developing countries in future one day in possible. I shal indicate the reasons as below:

The effects of climate change will not be uniformly distributed across the globe and there are likely to be winners and losers as the planet warms. Applying a broad brush to climate effects, developing countries are more likely to disproportionately experience the negative effects of global warming. Not only do many developing countries have naturally warmer climates than those in the developed world, they also rely more heavily on climate sensitive sectors such as agriculture, forestry and tourism. As temperatures rise further, regions such as Africa will face declining crop yields and will struggle to produce sufficient food for domestic consumption, whilst their major exports will likely fall in volume. This effect will be made worse for these regions if developed countries are able to offset the fall in agricultural output with new sources, potentially from their own domestic economies as their land becomes more suitable for growing crops. Moreover, developing countries may also be less likely to create drought resistant harvests given the lack of research funding.

Wild weather weighs on economies

The increased frequency and severity of extreme weather will weigh on government budgets. The aftermath of natural disasters often falls on authorities who are forced to spend vast amounts on clear-up operations and healthcare costs that come with experiencing extreme weather. Revenue reductions may also be experienced by countries heavily dependent on tourism or on selling fishing rights, fo

The effects on negative environment influence to developed countries and developing countries

As developed countries face an increasing strain on domestic budgets, fewer resources in the form of aid and economic development funds will flow to developing countries. The governments of these nations will be forced to channel resources away from productive and growth-enhancing projects towards countering the costs of extreme weather. Such effects will damage near-term growth prospects. Furthermore, developing countries are likely to have less capacity to rebuild. The time required to recover from natural disasters will be prolonged and if longer than the frequency in which such disasters occur, many developing economies could remain in a constant state of reconstruction.

Africa and Asia most at risk

Highly vulnerable regions in the emerging world include Sub-Saharan Africa and South and South East Asia, according to the World Bank. In South Asia, cities such as Kolkata and Mumbai will face increased flooding, warming temperatures and intense cyclones. Loss of snow melt from the Himalayas will also reduce the flow of water into the Indus Ganges and Brahmaputra basins. Meanwhile in South East Asia, Vietnam's Mekong Delta, which produces most of the rice, is especially vulnerable to rising sea levels. For Sub-Saharan Africa, food security will be a major challenge due to droughts and shifts in rainfall. Many developing nations are situated in low latitude countries and it is estimated that 80% of the damage from climate change may be concentrated. Consequently, higher agricultural yields, lower heating requirements and lower winter mortality rates are a handful of economic benefits climate change may bring, although these benefits may diminish as warming continues.

However, the prediction that developing countries will be disproportionately affected is reinforced by Standard and Poor's research on the influence climate change will have on sovereign risk. Recognising that climate change is a global mega-trend impacting sovereign risk through economic, fiscal and external performance, they find that lower-rated sovereigns appear most exposed. Based on these measures we can interpret the results in part as the susceptibility of an economy to climate change.

How poor climate change influences UK developed growth

In the UK, the average temperature is now 1°C higher that it was 100 years ago and 0.5°C higher than it was in the 1970s. As a higher latitude country, it is believed that the UK will fare better than many developing nations as global warming progresses. That is not to say the nation will escape the costs of climate change - particularly given its significant coastline where rising sea levels pose an obvious threat. According to scientists estimate of the cost of floods to the UK economy as a result of 3°C - 4°C of warming are in the region of 0.2% - 0.4% of GDP annually by the middle of the century, if flood management efforts are not strengthened.

In England, the south and parts of Yorkshire and Humberside are forecast to experience the greatest impact from flooding by 2050 . Aside from increased flooding, water availability will become progressively more constrained and droughts more frequent .Milder winters and the associated decline in cold-related mortality rates will be countered by a greater prevalence and severity of heat waves, bringing with it a higher number of heat-related mortalities. Finally, with the agricultural sector contributing approximately just 0.6% of GDP, the benefits of longer growing seasons will be marginal to the economy.

In conclusion, climate change may also indirectly affect the UK economy through global supply chains. The UK may both export to and import from climate-sensitive countries. The subsequent influence of climate change in these economies may feed through to the domestic economy through lower demand for exports or higher prices of imports.

V
Factors Influence Human Future High Technological Development Failure

Why do developed countries need to improve on culture, education, medical technologyl development aspects?

I shall attempt to explain that why America, Japan, England and India these four countries ought need to improve on above sevearal aspects as below:

Firstly, I shall explain that why Japan still needs to improve itself country technology development, although Japan had been a technological mature development country in long time. In Japan technological development history, Japan had owned high technological development on technological products manufacture aspect, such as electronic rice cookers, artificial intelligent rice cookers cars, televisions etcl technological products. But when Germany had also began to develop high technological products in global technological prodict market. In basic, all any similar Japan technological products. Germany had also owned high technological skills to manufacture to sell in global high technological products marekt.

So, nowadays, Germany may still be Japan's high technological product main competitor. It means that global homeholders technology products consumers, car buyers must choose any Germany and Japan high technological products to compare which are better quality in order to satisfy their useful need.s Hence, in global high technological products market, Japan won't be still high technological product leader as past history. If Japan did not continue to improve its technology, Germany will be the future high technology product leader to replace Japan, hence Japan can not neglect to consider how to continue to improve its technology development.

IN the past, science and technology in Japan is focused in vehicle manufacture technology, consumer electronic, robotics, medical devices, space exploration and film industry. For example, Japan's focus on intensive mathematics education and the reverence for engineers in Japanese culture aids enginnering talent development which as produced advances in automative engines, television display technology, videogames , optical clocks etc. On aerospace exploration aspect Japan had conducted space and planetary research., aviation research and development of space and satellites. On nuclear power development technology, since 1973, Japan has been looking to become less dependent on imported fuel and start on depend on nuclear energy. On electronic development aspect, Japan is well known for its electronic industry throughout the world, and Japanese electronic products account ofr a large share in the world market. However, Japan had beed a leading nation in scientific research, particularly biomedical research.

However, all of above technology, Germany will own advance technology to replace Japan to develop its products to sell to global easily. Germany had innovated its technology, e.g. the self -driving cars of the near future depend on precise digital geolocation data to navigate to arrive at destinations. So, Germany's non-manual driving vehicles innovation may be future nay countries car users' suppliers. Also, its battery technology is also one of future high technology mission 2021. Germany government began to support the construction of autonomous capacities in battery cell production to secure technological maximally exploit the battery calue chain. Germany government should continue to support electronic battery cell manufacturers, to drive force in the growing market for electronic cars and the goals of continuing to build their motors in Germany in the future.

Is Germany technology advanced? I believe that it is true, in the index's eighth edition for 2020, Germany was named the most technologically advanced nation, followed by South Korea, and Singapore, Germany is most known for its engineering, different high technological invention etc. aspect. Why is Germany so technologically advanced? Because Germany had been an academic powerhouse for a long time and as such education is focused on technological aspect. It's education goal is for good ideas to be translated quickly into innovative products and services. Moreover, Germany also considers Hyper automation, the distributed cloud, technological development. Some technological leaders predict the future high technological development countries may include: China, South Korea, United States , Singapre , United Kingdom, Russia, Japan and Germany .

The possible number or rank technological development countries rank may be 1 South Korea rank 2 ,ay be United States, rank 3 may be Japan, rank 4 may be Sweden nowadays. However, Germany may be future rank 1 technological leader, because Germany is so good at engineering. Germany's engineers borne out of the country are world leaders in their field, reowned for their dedication to precision, function and power. Over the years, Germany engineers have maintained their reputation to help Germany technology development products to as a top exporter of machinery and industrial equipment.

Moreover, in human development history, Germany are smart, when Germans are the most intelligent people in Europe, the British have an edge over rivals in France when it comes to the grwy matter , a new league of IQ scores has shown. The scored 94 and Germans were tap of the table with an IQ of 107, according to Richard Lynn, who headed the study. However, why is German technology will be the best. The major factor for Germany's success is that it has managed to homegrown scientific research and expertise to move up the technological ladder, concentrating on innovative products and processes not easily copied or undercut by cheap wages. The textile industry is a case in point, hence it causes that future Germany's technology development may be Japan's future one main competitos in technological product development market. So, it is right time, Japan needs to continue to research its new technological invention in order to improve its technological development to be the best to compare other high technological development countries.

Secondly, I shall discuss that why US needs to improve or change itself country's culture to let many different countries people can adopt to live. For example, nowadays, COVID 19 illness is serious to influence any one country people live. IN fact, US ia a developed country, it is global countries only one leader to encourage different countries people to live. Also, US is one comfortable living people to let global immigrants to feel. But, when COVID 19 disease occurred, some US people feel that it is possible due to

Chinese people , they contact COVID 19 disease to cause many US people get this kind of disease. However, it is none evidence to prove this kind of illness may be caused by Chiese to cause many US people die. So, US, opening culture began to change worse, e.g. some US people began to hate overseas immigrants to live itself country, it is possible due to many US people feel afraid to contact overseas immigrants, they may bring COVID 19 disease in their bodies, so when US people they contact these overseas COVID 19 disease immigrants, they may get this kind of disease . SO, it seems that US people's opening accept to let overseas immigrant living policy has changed to prohibit them to immigrate to live US easily.

However, I feel that US 's closing culture mind can not bring its social development to improve more easily. US ought to change its social culture has more opening cultural mind as before how it accepted different countries immigrants to choose US to live. Hence, it brings this question: What challenges US may encounter if it can be change its new cultural mind to accept more overseas immigrants to live easily? The challenges may include: American needs to understand themselves value and learn about what is important to Americans know why Americans value independence, equality and being on time. Americans will need see they are direct and informal and why competition, work ethic, and buying things are important in the US. American probably had strong traditions and culture that they valued. In the UNited States, there are also important American values are the things that are most important to Americans. For example, one of the main American values is independence. Independence is sometimes referred to US individualism. Americans are very proud of being self reliant, or being able to take care of themselves. American children tend to leave the home earlier than in oterh cultures, if they continue to live at home, they might be asked to pay rent or contribute to the house. So, Americans expect anyone who is able to work to do in order to support themselves. Also, Americans value privacy and their own space, when in some cultures wanting privacy may be seen as a bad thing, many Americans like to have alone time and may be private abour certain topic. In conversations, many Americans are private about certain things and do not want to talk about them, such as age, how much money they make, or their political, sexual and religious views. Americans often give each other more space in public situations than people in other cultures . They tend to stand with a bit of space between them, typically the distance of direct. This means that they often tell you what they think and they will be assertive about when they want.

Some peoples of American-style directness,, such as in conversation, if an American disagrees with youropinion, they might tell you, this does not mean they do not like you, just that they may have a different area. In classes, Americans may challenge their teachers' ideas. IN some culture, it is impolite to disagree with your teacher, it is never is rude to ask for help. Most Americans love to help and need very little encouragement to become good friends and neighbors.

However, I feel that America has lose equality value. Although, many newly immigrants moved to America to follow American team. They believed that if you worked hard, you could move up in society. But, today, more and more people realize the American dream is not true. Many people who work very hard do not have very much money. Often people who love from privileged backgrounds have an easier time moving up in the world. Still, the idea of equality is an important part of US culture.

So, COVID 19 disease occurrence had explained that US began have inequality culture difference causes, discrimination to overseas immigrants, e.g. Chinese. Americans discrimination behavior began to cause. American ought change itself new culture to traditional culture to accept different countires clever immigrants skills, talent people mind in order to help itself country to continue develop more advanced society to be world leader position.

Thirdly, I shall discuess why England needs to improve education. What negative impacts will happen, if UK does not continur improve education as well as its neglect on improvement education, how it will bring negative impact to its studetns minds in society? Why growth is the key to improve UK education development? Conventional wisdom states that smaller schools provide students with a better education . But studies of education systems around the world, show that growing schools could actually solve UK's poor student outcomes.

Nowadays, the UK's school system is in trouble, despite the fact that the last two decades have seen massive changes in the UK's education sector. UK education report indicated that in the past 15 years, the UK's four countries have spent $550 UK billion on operating and enhancing their secondary schools. IN the same period, England alone closed 35% of its schools (1,500 institutions) and opened almost 2,000 new ones . Nonetheless, little has improved UK education report indicated that in 2026, only 65% of all English pupils graduated with five or more grade as compared with 50% 15 years ago, at a cost od $37 billion per percentage point of improvement. The US was as a wholw spent the 8 th largest amount of 34 OECD countries, but only came, 19 th in mathemactics, 16 th in reading and 14 th in science.

So, what 's going wrong to cause UK students have worse learning performance. The reasons may include: Neglecting all four nations education reforming. Education in the UK is devolved to the four nations that make up the British union. For this reason, most of qualifications data relates only to England, although total spending figures are mostly UK wide. Academy shcools are amodel of schooling that is available only in England. There is no provision for the model in the other three nations of the UK.

The next reason is failure educational strategy. UK education report also indicated that England's strategy over the past 15 years has been to try to improve its education system by fixing its low lights , less than a third of students graduate with five or more GCE grade , reducing their projected lifetime earnings by $140,000. By putting their schools into " special measures" and offering them up for tender to other schools, it hopes that whole education system would improve. BUt, it has not . THe English have thrown more money at the proble,, spending 84% more on each child's education . Then, they did 15 years ago ($57,000 rather than $31,000), but although half their schools have improved, the other half have declined, and the overall picture is still the same. So, there are still many UK schools can not get UK government help to improve all school students individual learning effort to be better.

● What would have happened if UK government had spent the last 15 years trying to grow their education system bright lights, rather than brighten , their low lights?

UK education improvement strategy is such that a similar change in strategy helped the charity save the children reduce malutrition by 80% in Vietnam over two years, after decades of getting. Instead of trying to solve the poor learning ability of student learning performing problems in their worst areas, UK educators also need to expand a similar improvement education on strategy shift in order to help transform to UK any schools reforming educational policies in success.

Hence, if England had adopted another long term countrywide educational strategy, where all schools work together to improve standards across the UK in order to access all schoools resources, facilities and entracurricular activities and it could shown that good teachers in both schools can teach anyone. Then, most of UK teachers can know their subject inside out and quickly adapt their teaching methods to different needs. Consequently, when UK can imporve most of UK students learning effort to the best performance, as better educated students are more knowledgeable, money when they can attribute their the best effort to their society in the future. Then, UK society can be developed to reach the most top level, because UK's future development must depend on its next generation's help. If future UK education can train many talent students to attribute to social different aspects, such as technology, medical , business, construction etc. different professional aspects . UK future social development may be improved to be better to compare present society development. So, UK government can not neglect how to improve all UK student individual learning performance in order to help every UK student to pursue their abilities to prepare to attribute to UK future society devleopment successfully.

Finally, I shall discuss why India will need to improve medical technology. Recently, world news reported that INdia has many people are killed by COVID 19 disease. India is the highest population country. I assume that COVID 19 disease causes many Indians die because India has no enough hospitals, clinics to provide good medical quality to serve these COVID 19 disease contact patients. Due to lack of the best medical skillful doctors and nurses. So, many COVID 19 disease patients can not be saved to their lifes, even in India society, many none of COVID 19 disease contact people, when they contact to the COVID 19 disease people, they can not give good drugs to save themselves lifes. SO, it explains why India has many people are killed by COVID 19 disease in short time . SO, it seems that India lacks enough drugs to supply to these COVID 19 disease patients to cause there are many COVID 19 disease patients die in short time.

This COVID 19 diease attracks India matter occurs, it brings these questions: IS short time shortage of drug supply factor or long time shortage of drug supply factor to cause many COVID 19 disease patients die? Can long time poor medical technology factor cause many Indians die? IS COVID 29 disease the main factor causes many Indians die? India has many people are living. So, India must eed to improve its medical technology in order to solve the number increasing of India people future health challenge. One of the most important and highly debated, elements of India society is the quality of healthcare available to patients. The use of technology increases provider capability and patient access when improving the quality of life for some India clients and saving the lives of others. The India technology role can play in improving health of India. It can help in early detection of health problems. It cn also help in data collected from tests instantly monitor, the conditon of the patient, and then relay that information to the doctors and staff of the overall healthcare system.

However, the factors have made improvement in health conditions possible in India , they may include: A downtrend in communicable diseases, a focus on prevention , reduced neonatal mortality rates, tacking antimicrobial resistance, improved nutrition, using digital health and artificial intelligence for social impact, stronger government accountability. A number of industry analysts have observed that increased accessibility of treatment is one of the most tangible ways that technology has changed healthcase. Health IT opens up may more avenues of exploration and research, which allows experts make helathcare more driven and effectve than it has ever been. Hence, future India may apply these new medical technology, e.g. virtual reality, precision medicine, health wearables, artificial organs, 3D printing, wireless brain sensors, robotic surgery, smart inhalers, they are the main treatment option for asthma and if taken correctly, will be effective for 80% of India patients.

Hence, India must need solve medical technology improvement challenge in order to keep many people lifes , in special for the talent youngers, e.g. doctors, scientists, architects, lawyers, accountants , atc. professionals. I believe that India's medical technology can not been improved to raise quality in order to save many COVID 19 disease patents their lifes. So, many of COVID 19 disease patients can not been saved by good quality if medical drugs in short time. So, if INdia does not hope to lose many young talent professionals, it must need to continue improve its medical technology as soon as possible.

● How can our future social development can be improved ?

Nowadays, globalization cooperation or our societies become one society to any countries leaders is needed. I believe that countries competition will be serious, even we shall attack other countries if any one country can not accept " globalization cooperation mind". I mean that it is only globalization cooperation one way choice, then our societies can be improved or will be become better more easily.

For China and America two countries example, recently, because COVID 19 disease caused many Western and Asia countries began feel that COVID 19 disease was caused from Chinese. However, they have no evidence to indicate that COVID 19 disease must be caused from China. Although, before the year end of two years, there are some Chinese had ever travelers to US, then US had many people began to get this kind COVID 19 disease to cause many American die, when they did not believe that COVID 19 disease can cause human dies easily. Until to now, global many people had gotten this kind of illness to vause they die, when the health person contacts the owned COIVD 19 disease sick people . Although some people can be saved after they are saved by drug, but many people can not be saved, when they can not been saved by drug, even they still can not saved after they had been gotten drug. Such as US, UK, India, China, Germany , Korea, Japan, France these countries reported that they had many people could not saved to keep their lifes when they could not believe that they can get COVID 19 disease when they contact to the strange people who may owned COVID 19 diesease easily, when they are sitting down to the same table to eat in restaurants or when the COVID 19 disease strange person and the health person are talking together closely.

So, I believe that it is right time to any countries leaders need to act and to cooperate to find the method to avoid COVID 19 disease attacks any people. I mean the globalization cooperation attitude may nee to ourselves countries leaders . Our country leader can not only consider himself/herself country benefit and neglact to consider other countries benefits. If global humans hope that we can still to improve our culture to be peace or improve our space technology artificial intelligent development manufacturing to the advance level rapidly, or improve our medical technology to the best quality or improve our students learning effort or teachers teaching performance to reach the most satisfactory need to our future any one students. It is only global cooperation way to achieve global improved societies aim. If our societies or any one country leader still only consider how to protect himself/herself country businessmen benefits and leader himself/herself benefits, and rich people benefits , but they neglect to consider any one citizen benefits ,e.g. the low education, poor old age people, low income people in societies.Then, unfair and discrimination will be encouraged to occur in any one country society . Consequently when any one country low education , low income , poor old people can not feel comfortable to lieve in themselves countries. They will feel angry to complain themselves countries governments and leader individual ambitious behavior to influence these group people feel unhappy to live long time in themselves countries.

Consequently, the country's social education level will only continue to worse, even economy will continue recession, as ell as and kind of technologies won't continue improve. Due to our future any one country leader can not keep globalization cooperation mind or positive opening attitude to let any one itself country citizen feels comfortable to live forever. Then, the developed country ,e g. US, UK will not still keep technology development leading position easily. It is possible due to they only consider themselves social benefits, during this COVID 19 disease had been attacking themselves countries. So, they ought also consider other countries , they are attacked by COVID 19 disease, hoe to avoid COVID 19 disease will continue to attack any one country easily.

Hence, we only cooperate to help ourselves to find the best long time method to fight COVID 19 disease . When our countries leaders can cooperate to spend time to sit down to discuss how to fight COVID 19 disease , then I believe that our global societies may been improved more better rapidly as soon as possible in this year.

● Methods to avoid future human developmend failure

Finally, I shall conclude that how we can avoid human development failure. we need to know that human is facing threat of self-benefit behavior. We can follow our development to analyze why we shall encounter failure of improvement stage in our soon future. In our past thousand years, human had developed in success from fishing, agriculture stage till to manufacture industry innovation stage, till to nowadays high technological development stage ,even our future artificial intelligent high technology (non-manual control machine stage). Although all of our past development , till to nowadays development, it seems that we can develop in success in any technological aspects ,e.g. space, computer , internet , ecommerce , medical technology etc. even future non-manual control (AI) artificial intelligent technology. But, some ways may help us to continue high technological development in success, even damage our future continue high technological development. They may include unfriend or poor culture development, lacking globalization cooperation, self -beefit mind factors.

All of above factors are any countries leades self-benefit mind or negative attitude (human behavior) to influence our future high technology continue development can succeed in possible. The reason is because that if any one country leader only considers how to protect himself/herself country technological development beefit, it means that he/she does not allow his/her country talent scientists can discess their any new technological invention opinions to let other countries talent scientists to learn ho to improve themselves new technological invention together. This point is the main bad factor to cause human future any kinds of high technological development to delay in possible, because our any kinds of high technological development success, we must depend on global scientists can have chance to share their any kinds of new technological experiments to let they can learn why the scientist can develop the kind of product in success, or why the scientist can not develop the kind of product in success. Then, any one country scientists can absorb other countries scientists their successful or failure scientific experiements in order to improve their any kinds of new technological expeiment to achieve the most satisfactory scientific experiement demand to bring benefit to us. So, globalization cooperation is the only way to avoid human development failure absolutely.

● Why do developed countries need to continue to learn how to improve new technology ?

In fact, there are different between developing and developed countries. Developing countries, such as Afria, Korea, China, Taiwan, these countries are developing, so their IT information , medical, manufacturing technology, artificial intelligence etc. different industries are not mature, they must need to continue improvement to develop their skills in order to satisfy consumers market need. Because social need had been often changing, so these developing countries scientists, businessmen need to have good learning mind to prepare to learn how technological , medical , artificial intelligent, IT knowledge in order to satisfy consumer individual new product useful need and keep market competitive effort in themselves home an overseas consumption markets both more easilu. But, why do developed countries also need to continue to learn how to improve new technology? What negative impacts will bring to developed countries their scientists and businessmen do not continue to improve their new products development or continue to research how to improve their old products to achieve the best quality to order consumers needs.

Nowadays, global consumption market competition is serious. Consumer individual need or demand is increasing, when one consumer feels the kind of old product can not satisfy his/her actual need, he/she will seek to find which brands of products, they have similar function or useful characteristics in order to make comparison to other similar kinds of products. Then, he/she will make final purchase decision. So, when the consumer had habit to use the brand of product, it does not mean that he/she will continue to use this brand of product. He/she may be influenced to change to choose the another brand of similar function characteristics of new product to buy use in this rapid changing competitive market.

Hence, if the developed country's culture is changed to closing mind from opening mind. These developed country, such as US people can not accept to other countries people new, useful, attributing innovativ mind of ideas easily. They only consider or recognite that themselves ideas are the best or the most useful. Consequently, due to their foolish closing minds, their traditional protection themselves believes will cause difficult to continue to improve or develop, because it is possible that there are any other developed countries, e.g. UK, Germany, Japan, they have some talent people, scientists their technological skills may be proficient or more advanced to compare US, itself countries some scientists.

So, I recommend that any developed countries can not only consider to appreciate themselves countries scientists must be the most smart to compare other developed countries. Any one developed country scientists ought need to cooperate with other developed countries scientists to discuss or research any new invention together in order to help themselves technology can been improved rapidly in order invent many different kinds of new products to satisfy consumers themselves often changing useful needs in this global consumption market nowadays.

This developed country Japn is one good example to explain that why its scientists ought need to continue to improve their different technology or science skills as well as learn any new kinds of technology or science knowledge from other developed countries scientists , such as US, UK, Germany together. Because it is only one effective technology and science improvement method (way) to Japan scientists,when they can accept the other developed scientists different new or innovated opinions as well as they can spend some time to sit down to discuss and cooperate to help themselves old products how to change or innovate new products in order to attract global consumers purchase choice. So, although, Japan had been one developed country long time, its technology development had searched mature stage in the past, But, it can not reprsent that its technology must be more advanced to compare other developed countries, such as UK, US, Germany. Because these any one developed country, their scientists still continue carry on researching how to improve themselves old products to be new. So, it seems that Japan's any old technological products, e.g. smart phones, television, washing machines, rice coolers, products won't bring more attract to persuade global consumers choices. Because US, UK, Germany etc. different developed countries scientists had began to research how to continue improve its traditional old technological products to be more attraction in order to adopt global technological products users needs. For example, developing country India, due to its medical technology is poot, if it hopes to improve itself country technology, it must need to attempt to concentrate on spending money, medical teaching resources on medical technology aspect. India's medical technology improvement must be any kinds of technologies , the most need to improve to compare IT technology, manufacturing technology, artificial intelligent technology, space technology etc. The reason is that India is the highest population country, if its medical technology's cost, it will cause many young talent people die, such as COVID 19 disease occurs to India recently. It causes many Young talent Indians die, due to it lasks enough good medical technology to supply drugs to save them. So, if India government hopes that it can have many talent high skillful technology youngers to serve itself country. It will need to consider how to improve its medical technology in order to fight any possible new kind of illness attack, instead of COVID 19 disease, when India can improve its medical technology to save many young talent scientists' lifes . Then, it won't lose many talent scientists and they can continue to attribute themselves scientific knowledge for India itself country lont time technological science development.

Hence, UK and US both governments need to consider how to allocate enough land to supply to any manufacturing and business operations efficiently, how to help any educational organizations to train talent employees and school organizations to teach talent students, how to supply enough loan to assist any business founders to develop their new businesses in success or create new entrepreneurship. All of these can bring advantages to satisfy their societies needs.

Economists generally agree that highly economic development and growth are influenced by four factors: Human resources, physical capital, natural resource and technology. So, in general, US an UK countries hope they can become highly developed countries have government that focus on these areas. They mean that factors may influence one developed country to continue to become highly developed country, factors may include: accumulation of capital stock, increases in talent labor inputs, such as workers or hour worked, technological advancement. All of these factors may assist UK , US continue to bring highly development benefit. So, UK, US are such as industrialization in developed countries, they need to improve these industrial productivity in order to continue to keep, highly developed countries in possible, these factors may include: long term technological development, improvement quality of human resources, encough availability of finace, efficient managerial talent, efficient government policy and surplus of enough supply of natural factor, e.g. good climate for agriculture, enough natural coal , land natural resource supply. However, they also need to consider these are negative factors to affect them to continue develop, e.g. lack of drive of social motivation for improvement, unproductive social functions, such as war or having very large family sizes, negative social cultures, such as gambling and drinking wine, and lack of skills due to poor training and education . They may be poor social negative factors to influence they continue develop in success.

VI

Robotic future development how to influence developing and developed countries societies

Nowadays, since electronic vehicle invention, it brought competition to fight traditional gas vehicle martet. Electronic vehicle is only needed to be charged battery, then battery will bring energy to push the electornic car to be driven fastly. So traditional vehicle market is experiencing decline life cycle stage. When, electronic vehicle is popular to be accepted to every drivers. In fact, when we drive cars on the roads, our cars will have gas emission to polluate our sir. Earth warmth is dramatically increasing. The main reason is that global air is polluted, e.g. frequent driving activities will bring air pollution when gas emission is caused. Hecnce, environment vehicle is only needed to charged battery. Every time battery charged can bring one day driving time power or enerty to let drivers to drive . So, basing on environmental protection and battery long time driving both reasons, it brings strengths to electronic vehicle to persuade global any drivers to choose to buy electronic vehicle more than traditional gas vehicle.

I shall research these questions: These questions may concern: Will the gas vehicle be influenced to experience the decline life cycle stage rapidly when the electronic vehicle is accepted to be popular to drive ? Can traditional gas vehicle avoid decline life cycle stage comes as well as if traditional gas vehicle real prepares to experience decline life cycle stage ? Can it re-grow to change to enter growth life cycle stage again? Can new electronic vehicle market influence traditional gas vehicle market to shorten time to experience decline life cycle age rapidly?

In our driving history, cars invention had helped us do not need to spend long walking time to go to anywhere conveniently. In fact, due to technological limit, e.g. bus, taxi, tram, train must use gas to be energy to push them to be driven on the roads. When car invention period, or it may call car market birth life cycle stage period. In the 1800 year beginning , human does not know what car function or why we need car. When cars had been invented, it is global whole car industry borth life cycle stage period. This period its characteristics are: In societies , people accepted car tools to drive on the roads. Many people feel to spend money to buy cars, it is waste money, because they may choose to catch any kinds of public transport tools, e.g. bus, train, tram, taxi, ferry, undergroundtrain to arrive any destinations conveniently. So, from 1800 year to 1900 year, global whole car industy had been still keeping in the growth life cycle stage. Because in global society, many people hasd been general accepting public tranposrt tools, their fee are vey cheap and passengers can spend short time to catch them to go to anywhere, they can provide long transport service time for office working people, student from morning to evening time. Hence, this 100 years period, global car sale number could not significant increase, because public transport tools could bring convenience to any one when they needed to leave homes to arrive far away destination in short time.

Hence, global car industry ought not develop rapidly, because many peoplecould not accept to spend money to buy cars to replace to catch any public transport tools. But after 1900 year, global whole gas vehicle industry began to experience growth life cycle stage. Because global many people had jobs to do, unemployment ratio begain to reduce. In society, rich people number began to increase. It based on theseboth factors: families began to consider to attempt to buy any kinds of cars in order to attempt to buy any kinds of cars in order to let them to feel enjoyable to drive to go to anywhere. So, from 1901 year to 2000 year, it may be global whole gas vehicle market growth life cycle stage . In this period, global car buyers number had been increasing significantly . In average, global every family may own at least one car, even more. It depends on whether how many members number, the family has and whether the family has how many member(s), he/she has own one car licence. Moreover, in society, many people began to accept second hand cars, because second hand cars must be chaper to compare new cars as well as it is real one good choice for the low income car buyer social consumer groups in society. So, in this global vehicle market growth life cycle stage, instead of new car buyers number had been increasing significantly, the second hand car buyers number had also been increasing significantly in the same time. So, global new cars and secod hand car buyers number had increased rapidly every year, because global population is increasing. It also caused many working people did not like to spend long time to queue to wait public transport tools, it is another factor to persuade people chooce to buy cars to drive to go to offices or schools or anywhere in their relax time, e.g. holiday, sunday. So, this 100 year, may be global whole car industry growth life car cycle stage.

After 2000, it may be global car industy mature life cycle ctage , many car manufacturers begun to innovate any kinds of traditional cars to change to advanced engine function, auto-window, auto dooe functions , navigation road locaion search function, even non-manual driven artificial intelligent car invention. So, after 2000 year, due to global car buyers begun to pursue comfortable drivin feeling. They need to pursue comfortable driving feeling. They need to buy unique design of cars, or more functions of cars to drive on the road . Hence, global different unique function and styles of cars purchase needs had been significant increasing. Moreover, car prices had also been increasing more, due to more different unique functional and styles of car purchase needs had been increasing in order to satisfy the rich or high income car buyers group. So, after 2000, it may be global car market 's mature life cycle stage.

But, I believe that global car market's mature life cycle stage can not keep long time. The main reason is because the electronic car invention. After 2000 year, since one kind of new transport tool of electronic car invention, it influences many gas car owners or non car owners feel interesting to learn how to drive electronic cars and feel whether what advantages that electronic cars can satisfy their driving needs. IN special, environmental protection awareness drivers must believe electornic cars can reduce air pollution when they choose to drive them on the roads , due to none gas emission effect to pollute our earth air. When they choose to drive electronic cars, due to they only need to charge battery, then their electronic cars can be driven on the roads in short time rapidly. Even, report also indicated driving electronic cars accident occurrence chance may be also influenced to reduce to compare driving gas cars usually. So, electronic vehicle market may be future main competitor to global traditional gas vehicle market.

May electronic vehicle invention influence future gas vehicle shorten time to experience to decline life cycle stage rapidly? How gas vehicle market may avoid the shorten time to experience decline life cycle stage if electronic vehicle market may influence its development in global car manufacture industry? I shall attempt to solve these challenges as below:

IN fact, electronic vehicle innovation is not long time , so the global electronic vehicle manufacturing and sale market is experiencing birth life cycle stage. Can electronic vehicle market reduce to shorten time to experience growth, even mature life cycle stages. It depends on these factors: The factors may affect battery electronic vehicle energy consumption and driving behavior impact. They may include whether environment protection awareness will increase or decrease to global nay one gas car owners or non car owners. Because if global environment protection awareness increase, it will influence gas car owners or non car owners (potential either battery electronic vehicle energy or gas vehicle energy car choice buyers), begun to feel their frequent driving gas vehicle behaviors may bring air pollution or global warming, temperature rises weather disaster occurrence in the future. They alsoknow battery electronic vehicle energy consumption price may be cheap to same to gas vehicle energy consumption. Moreover, they may feel that if they change to drive battery electronic vehicles, it may help them to minimize environmental air pollution impacts of the end of life stage and brings positive impacts on improving climate change and air quality for our future. So, if many car owners or non car owners feel that they have responsibility to protect our climate environment pollution. Then, battery electronic vehicle buyers number will have possible to increase rapidly in short time. Due to the significant impact of gas vehicle and battery electronic vehicle their life cycle analysis can be utilized to analyze the advantages and disadvantages to cause car buyers make comparison between them and gas vehcile and battery electronic vehcile both kinds vehicles are highly complex supply chain choice in the automobile industry nowadays. Moreover, due to carbon intensity of this stage was calculated from emission factors at the global car manufacture industry. Hence, emission factor may be one important influential factor to influence any one makes car purchase decision or either gas or battery electronic car purchase decison.

For example , in our societies, if many peopl own environment protection awareness, then global gas vehicle buyers number may be influenced to reduce, even the owning gas vehicle families may be influenced to choose to buy battery electronic cars to replace their gas cars. They may sell their gas vehicles to any one, even to steel manufacturers easily. Hence, gas vehicle on steel existence number may also reduce ot they can disappear in our road in short time rapidly. If batttery electronic vehcile can be popular to accept to drive on the road to any one driver in our societies. Then, battery electronic cars may be influenced to increase driving needs to any one driver. it's sale number may also influenced to increase rapidly. Consequently, it may have chance to experience to growth life cycle stage from birth life cycle stage in short time rapidly in global whole electronic car manufacturer and sale market.

Then another influential factor concerns how owning car consumers feel the charge of the battery energy use of resources in comparison to conventional gas energy use of resources to driving cars. In combination with the regional electricity mix these factors influence the energy materials for a specific car market. For these first life cycle phases a range of values is possible to battery electronic car market. If in our societies, there are many people choose to use battery charge energy resource to drive electronic cars, their prices are very reasonable to compare gas vehicles or they feel gas will face rapid shortage challenge, if global any one only likes to drive gas vehicle. Then, they may be influenced to choose to buy the battery electronic vehicles to replace gas vehicles. Hence, enery resource used to car my also be one main factor to influence any one car buyer individual either battery electronic car or gas vehicle purchase choice.

Hence, it implies that the life style environmental impacts and energy resource used both impacts of battery electronic cars are a topic of increasing relative importance of the vehicle production stage and the maximum impact on climate change (ingc02/km) that is observed by many climate scientists, their observation to climate change good or bad change effect may influence global battery electronic vehicle needs. So, how clean are battery electric cars, it will be one popular topic for environmental scientists to environmental protection awareness car owners and non car owners. T o analysis hoe to cause electric car life cycle changes. The arrival of the electric car has brought with it an array of life cycle factors that influence the carbon emission level to any one country's environment.

Influence of national electricity grid over the use phase, so it implies that if the country feels carbon emission level is high , due to gas vehicle may bring carbon emission to pollute air to the country. Although, factory's carbon emission or airplane carbon emisson may be one factor to influence the country's air pollution level to be increase. The year has high carbon emission level, it considers gas vehicle air carbon emission level whether it is high or low in the year. So, if the country's gas vehicle car owners number is sudden increasing rapidly. Consequently, it will evaluate that the car increasing number may influence the country itself carbon emission level to be high and it may cause air pollution seriously.

Hence, battery electric car industry life cycle whether when it can experience growth life cycle stage or mature life cycle stage from birth life cycle stage, it depends on what carbon emisson level to any one country. If this year has many countries believe their high carbon emissin level is due to gas vehicle 's carbon emission causes. Then, this high carbon emission level report factor may raise many car owners or non car owners consider environment protection awareness and it may also influence many car buyers choose to buy battery electric cars to replace gas cars to drive on the road frequently in this year.

Also in order to avoid themselves countries' air pollution is more serious. Hence, global carbon emission rise or fall level and any one environmental protection awareness psychological both factors may influence future battery electric car market development. They may have close relationship to influence any one traditional gas vehicle owner to buy one new battery vehicle vehicle to replace it to drive on the road, or any one potential car purchaser makes final battery electric car or gas vehicle decision absolutely. On conclusion, above these factors may explain whether it is possible that battery electronic vehicle invention may influence future gas vehicle market changes to decline life cysle stage from mature life cycle stage. It depends on whether environmental protection awareness to car owners increasing or decreasing number , carbon emission level whether it is high or low, gas energy resource facing shortage factors to influence future electronic vehicle need.

Management science solves public transport passenger queue problem Waiting Line (Queuing) Models: solution imbalanced taxi and passenger queue in urban public transportation service case

The Four Problems Of Urban Transportation (And The Four Solutions)
The fixed-route bus and the bicycle solve at least one urban problem better than new technologies urban transportation problem case. There are four main problems in urban transportation that require four separate solutions. Some urban transportation design recommendion argued that technology can solve some problems, but not the same problem that public transit solves."The city has four separate problems of urban transportation which have four separate kinds of solutions, and it is very important to not mistake the solution for one problem for the solution for a different problem."
The first solution :
Bus stop time real -time information technology and apps solution method
Friction arises between a transit system and its users when the users don't have the information they need when they need it. That problem has been largely solved, Walker said, by information technology and apps. "That has been a fantastic transformation. Some of you may not be old enough to remember what life was like without real-time information, when you just went right out into the snow and wondered when the bus was coming."
The second solution:
Innovation method
The innovation method solves the city has four separate problems of urban transportation may include: Emissions and Energy Efficiency: "for which we're currently working on electric vehicles, and that's fantastic." Labor and Safety: The cost of labor is the primary driver of operation costs for passenger transport, Walker said. "It is why your bus doesn't come more often, and it is also why Uber can't make money." Autonomous vehicles will address that and the accident rate. "There is a problem with the efficient use of labor, and also a colossal problem of safety for which we are talking about autonomous vehicles, and that's fantastic." Space: "And there is a fourth problem which is the efficient use of space, for which the solution is on the one hand, cycling and walking, and on the other, public transit provided by big vehicles."
The third soution:
The fixed-route bus or train solutione method is the best solution reason
The fixed-route bus or train is the vehicle of the future, because it remains the most efficient way to move large numbers of people through the congested space of a city. In his critique of public transit, Musk pointed out that people prefer "individualized transport, that goes where you want, when you want," like the Tesla Model S. But Walker contends individualized

transport that goes where you want when you want can't move people through a congested city as efficiently as a fixed-route bus.

"We are always going to need vehicles sized to the appropriate capacity requirement, which means big buses in big cities," he said. "Our friends in the tech industry, including many of you here, and I love what you're doing, are always trying to sell us stories about how everything will fit together into a magnificent fusion. They want us to mix it up, to think about how it combines. And I'm always saying, but wait a minute, if you're going to be a smart customer you have to think about how they work separately as well."

Instead of above technological methods to solve public transport problem. The queue control management method will be one good solution How do I conduct queue management of passengers in waiting taxi or bus area for Public transportation Vehicles?

Are there existing design projects and studies that a public transportation vehicle (Taxi or Bus) would know the number of passenger in waiting area/ shed through long range network? I am conducting a design project for buses in my country that would know the number of passenger in waiting area and this information will be sent to the terminal or bus which will they used to pick up these passengers. Thus, congestion of buses and passenger can be lessen

I think that there are 2 technical issues: a) how to collect and transmit information, b) how to manage public transportation to minimize queue. About the 1st question you probably need either to do it manually (operator sitting at every station and making phone calls like "please send one more bus urgently, we have 100 of people waiting here", but this may be too expensive, at least for city buses) or to do it automatically (video camera, some image recognizing software that calculates people and then sends a message to the center) in this city has four separate problems of urban transportation concerns taxi and bus queue case.

Conclusion of the best solution method

As I know, there is not such a system design yet. but you may devise one by using the queue theory and optimizing the performance of the system by the following pattern:

- defining a objective function corresponding to the total passengers awaiting time.

- optimizing the objective function by finding the best set of assigning the available buses to the stations (considering the routes)

Waiting Line (Queuing) Models: solution imbalanced taxi and passenger queue in airport case

Predicting Imbalanced Taxi and Passenger Queue Contexts in Airport management problem

For certain types of problems involving queues, special descriptive models have been developed to predict the performance of service systems such as car garages – cars standing in queue for servicing.

The taxi and passenger queue contexts indicate the various states of queues related to taxis and passengers (i.e. taxis are waiting for passengers, passengers are waiting for taxis, both are waiting for each other, none is waiting). Predicting these queue contexts in a future time is very important for better airport ground transport operations. However, queue context prediction at the airport is a challenging problem due to the presence of different contextual factors i.e., time, weather, taxi trips, flight arrivals and many more. Also these taxi and passenger queue contexts at the airport are imbalanced since some of the contexts are very infrequently occurring compared to others. In this paper, we address the problem of predicting imbalanced taxi and passenger queue contexts at the airport. First, we investigate different contextual factors, including time, taxi trips, passengers and weather for queue context prediction. Then we propose a detailed step by step solution to address this problem. To support the effectiveness of our detailed approach, we generate a queue context dataset by fusing three real world datasets including taxi trip, passenger wait time and weather condition that represent the taxi and passenger queue contexts at any major international airport in any country City. The experimental results demonstrate that our developed queue context prediction framework provides detailed solutions to deliver higher accuracy in queue context prediction.

Therefore, context-aware mobility analytics enables the provision of intelligent analysis on mobility contexts considering different user perspectives. The success of many applications such as transport management and location recom- mendation requires the discovery of valuable knowledge through extensive analysis of related factors . For example, an airport can be regarded as the first and last impression of a city. Since a longer passenger wait time for a taxi ride can diminish the satisfaction rating of an airport , the authorities try hard to maintain a higher customer satisfaction rating by providing various mobility services such as easy and comfortable airport transfer to the city using taxicabs. However, the demand-supply equilibrium of taxis is highly dependent on the taxi drivers' decisions to make airport trips. The ubiquitous data can help with managing the mobility of airport users by detecting different mobility contexts (i.e. situa- tions of the concurrent queues related to passengers and taxis) . The intelligent analysis and prediction of different mobility contexts can help with making mobility decisions for airport passengers and taxis at different times of the day.

We argue that by incorporating the temporal deviation of taxi drivers' moves as the feature importance score can identify good quality neighborhoods and thus significantly boost the taxi-passenger queue context prediction accuracy. We utilize a real world queue context data set that includes information from taxi trip logs, airport passenger arrivals and weather conditions which are relevant to the different queue contexts. Then we propose a temporal driver-knowledge deviation based feature importance scheme to select a quality neighborhood for predicting taxi and passenger queue contexts.

As we extract more features by computing the deviations of all feature values from its hourly mean along with the current features of the queue context dataset , it is necessary to check the relevancy of all features. The reason is that the use of all these features may degrade the prediction performance significantly due to the inclusion of some irrelevant and redundant features. Also, for different stations, the configurations such as lane numbers, and maximum queue length of taxis and passengers can affect the solution of the passenger-taxi queue problem.

The proliferation of pervasive devices in smart cities has enabled the development of many smart mobility applications . Smart parking is one of the innovations that provides easy to use parking services to the urban commuters by leveraging pervasive sensors and flexible payment systems.

Inferring a situational awareness map using clustering methods has become a popular research topic in recent years. GPS trajectory has been utilised in smart mobility applications. In this section, we briefly review the related work which can be separated into two categories: points clustering and trajectory clustering. For example, intelligent reminders of user activities and notifications for major transporta- tion delays due to the current situation of the users. This outcome can also be leveraged for the applications of discovering user rou- tines based on personal contexts of mobile users. In an intelligent healthcare scenario, a robust and simultaneous recogni- tion of multiple user contexts would be important to be considered for elderly and disabled people, while travelling through various accessible paths .

HOW DESIGNING UNDERGROUND MASS TRANSIT RAILWAY TO BRING PASSENGERS

● Designing transportation system advantages

Nowadays, transportation and economic development have close relationship. Economic development stimulates transportation demand by increasing the numbers of workers commuting to and from work, customers traveling to and from services areas, and products being moving by lorries on the roads between products and customers. According to Bailey, Mokhtarian and Little (2008) indicated "transportation route is past of distinct development pattern or road network and mostly described by regular street patterns as an important factor of human existence, development and civilization. The route network combined with increased road transportation investment result in changed levels of conveniently reflected through cost benefit analysis, savings in travel time, and other benefits. " These benefits are noticeable in increased catchment areas for services and facilities , shops, schools, offices, banks and leisure activities.

What are the crisis of neglection to care transporation system ? Why do any countries need to design road transportation system? For example, the Japan country lacks design road trsnaportation system effectively. So, the crisis of road traffic fatalities will raise and the econominc influence will be changed. The crisis indicates more than 7,000 people die annually as a result of motor vehicle crashes in Japan. Driving when under the influence of alcohol is the leading cause of motor vehicle crash fatalities in both developed and developing countries. So, alcohol is the most serious factor to raise personal risk when drivers are driving in Japan. However, a number of studies have shown that deterring drink driving is an important way to cause fatalities. There is a demonstrative need for social change in Japan.

Japan has recently strengthened its already strict laws in order to reduce the number of alcohol related road fatalities. Those deforms lowered the legal blood alochol contant limit increased, the penalties for offenders. The Japan road traffic legal needs. Any driving a motor with a alcohol limit of 0.03 or higher Japan's maximum sentence is up to 3 years imprisonment or a fine not exceeding 500,000 yen dollars. Is law impact to reduce drinking alcohol to drive in Japan? What are economic influence of the crisis of road traffic fatalities in Japan?

The rational choice theory of offending suggests that offenders are active decision makers who influence a large number of variables into decision whether or not to commit an offence. On the cost-benefit analysis, it is the punishment a possible jail, large fines worth is the reward the convenience of driving home without the expause of a taxi and innovenience to the alcohol drivers in Japan. Instead of law reforms when it detects alcohol in the air exhaled from the alcohol and other offenders and it educates children about the dangers of drinking and it also explains why alcohol driving can also threaten drivers' life when who are drinking alcohol and driving behaviour in the same time in Japan.

On the economic influence hand, implementation of the policy deregulating alcohol sales and alcohol production did not appear to increase traffic fatalities among adult or teenage males or females in Japan. We found that male adult fatalities demonstrated a statistically significant decline following enactment of the deregulation policy in 1994 year. So, Japan implement law to threaten alcohol drinking behaviour is useful. It can influence the alcohol availability and consumption, alcohol production and sales, the 24 hours operated convenience stores or liquor discount stores incomes to be reduced. Even, Japan overall GDP is also reduced from the deduction of liquor alcohol production and sale, also the occurrence of traffic accident fatalities chances will be also reduced.

The Japanese economy has entered a rapid process of liberalization since the mid-1990 year. Many sectors previously under direct government control are now regulated by the competitive market place. The Japanese alcohol beverage market has changed. The entry of cheaper import alcohol products resulted in a encouragement of alcohol consumption to Japan drinking drivers and an raising of increasing of more import alcohol products supply to Japan. Although, it is beneficial to Japan GDP growth. But it also raise the occurrence of chance to traffic accidents rate to cause alcohol drinkers to be death or hurt when who choose drinking alcohol to drive at the same time in Japan. So, alcohol import can bring more consumption, but it can also raise many traffic accidents occurrence in Japan in the same time.

In conclusion, alcohol is not good for health to drink when the consumer often buys alcohol at drink habitually. So, if many Japanese, including the alcohol driving consumers and the alcohol non drinking consumers both who often buy different countries alcohol to drink daily. It will cause their bodies to be unhealth for long term in Japan. It is possible to increase Japan's government's medical expenses to assist the low income or poor people in the future. So, although alcohol import can raise Japan GDP growth in the short term, but it also raise Japan government's medical expenditure to the low income or poor Japanese long term in the future, So it's economic benefit will not good in the future if Japan still import much alcohol to sell in its country.

Many commercial users depend on road transport facilities, with movement of products and services from place to place on the roads, aspect of global and urban economic survival. Hence, developments of various transportation modes have become important to physical and economic developments. For example, urban locations with such relative advantages are found where different transport routes with high degree of connectivity, within the intra and inter urban road networks. On similarly, commercial activities like banking, retail/wholesale businesses and professional services can take advantage of nearness to concentration of activities attracted consumers service providers. This partly caused increase in demand for commercial space and its effects on commercial property values along commercial roads can be rose. However, some countries' roads need to provide pedestrian movements more than the businesses activities, e.g. shorten the time of lorries parking on the road to let pedestrian movements on the narrow road. If the country government did not consider the roads need to let more pedestrian movements or shorten the time of lorries parking on the road. It will cause traffic jam or traffic density of the individual roads. Hence, governments need to concern the locations of commercial property buildings and the relationship between the explanatory variables of the design road networks.

What are construction of roads design networks benefits? In fact, construction of roads increased substantially with the opening up of residential environments that also is getting much benefits from increasing demand for spaces in commercial properties. Many private companies, retail stores, commercial banks aggregate in the main roads of cities, which get advantage of opportunities afforded by locations near central of cities to attract many pedestrians concerning their businesses existence. This led to high concentration of vehicular and pedestrian movements. Specially along the access main roads in the central of cities. The main roads exhibits linkages to form networks of minor routes along which commercial properties locate. If commercial users are displaced residential users, causing sites to be at the highest and best uses with increases in the values of commercial properties. However, it seems road network development is affected by the compact nature of various routes that sometimes causes volume of traffic jam. Thus, demand for transport can't be treated solely as a derived demand road. Improved main and minor roads access an city or rural areas is a necessary (but not sufficient). Precondition for increased productivity, the UK Standing Advisory committee On Trunk Road Assessment (SACTRA, 1999) noted "various ways in which transport can affect economic growth, for example benefits include through reorganization and rationalization of production, distribution and land use: reducing labor costs by expanding catchment areas etc."

What is land use and road transport design system relationship? Land use refers to the whole range of human activity and of the built environment, and to some aspects of the natural environment. This is a way relationship between land use and road transport. Governments need to design how to use land and how to design road transportation systems. e.g. where are built the main roads and/or where are built the minor roads are the most suitable locations in the cities or rural areas ? If the main roads is located in the not suitable locations at the centers of the cities or rural, it will case the increasing traffic volumes and levels of congestion, including air pollution, noise, ground water pollution from run-off , loss of soil functions and loss of bio-diversity to natural environment. By influencing the spatial structure of locations in the urban environment, so land use planning can help to mitigate any negative effects resulting from land use changes.

Modelling and land use transportation interactions has become an important aspect of road design transport planning. On the one side, for example, design roads in urban centers, it can increase land use and it can also reduce employees or students catching buses or driving cars' time spending to go to workplaces or schools users. Hence, the land use and roads designing transportation can give benefits to residents and employment people to reduce time to wait buses or taxies etc. public transportations to go to workplaces or schools or shopping centers etc. anywhere. It seems to assist bus companies or taxi drivers to earn more income, On the other side, designing urban transport systems is also important . Increased densities mean more destinations become within convenient walking and cycling distances and consequently the use of these modes tends to be higher. Also in dese cities public transport systems are able to offer higher levels of service and operate more economically, when the provision of sufficient road space to meet potential demand becomes impractical. It aims to reduce the danger of driving or walking in urban areas. The transport modes (that is walking, cycling, public transport) and the extent of car dependence is less, due to driving users dependency is less on rural roads. Hence, building main roads can concentrate on designing convenience to pedestrian walking to close to their houses on the streets. However, poor transport design and land use can cause to spend too expenditure not only transport costs on governments and transport users both and also the costs of providing other services. These include the usual utilities and also education and health services as well as negative externalities , such as greenhouse gas emissions. Most such studies concluded that there are significant financial and economics cost advantage of inner city redevelopment compared with fringe development.

However, such policies won't necessarily be successfully, in particular because of the two ways road problem, they may result in additional private investments and employment opportunities flowing into the region, buy may equally result in population and employment opportunities flowing out of the target region because of the improved access to other centers. Hence governments need to analyze how to arrange the land use to assist the property developers to choose where are the suitable locations to build offices or factories or shopping centers or houses at capital or urban cities to adapt to whose the growth of living population. For example, to judge where the land use whether where main roads or junior roads are built where are the suitable locations to satisfy the lorry drivers to park their lorries are the safe locations ; to design the minor roads to let the pedestrians to feel no danger to walk on the streets when the cars are driven to near to the streets on the minor roads. Thus, the factor of choosing where the land use to design the main or minor roads areas, sizes and lengths and of the minor or major roads can influence the drivers and pedestrians feel safe or dangerous when who are driving whose cars on the roads or who are walking on the streets to arrive the offices, schools, cinemas, church, houses etc. destination.

Designing road transportation networks how to assist economic growth ? I feel it is not all transport investments will be equally effective in enhancing economic growth. Designing road transport investment is a necessary, but on its own not sufficient requirement to earn significant economic growth at either a national or regional level. There are conditions under three categories: economic conditions, investment conditions and political conditions. In fact, although in some circumstances, transport investment may be a necessary condition for enhancing economic growth, it is rarely on its own a sufficient condition. Other factors including the broader policy environment, need to be present if the investment is going to be successful in addressing regional economic objectives. My some suggestions the following key aspects as being most relevant including:

a. Scale economies for example, where these dominate, lower transportation costs through improved accessibility may encourage increased concentration of firms in core regions, until the point that diseconomies set in.

b. Size of the local market.

c. Local land and labor conditions.

d. The nature and scale of transport improvements.

e. The nature of backward and forward linkages

in the country's local economy.

In any countries, road transportation improvements don't guarantee increased economic development. To increase economic development, an improvement needs to assist any lorry drivers to drive in short trips to reduce transportation costs and shorten time driving on the road or to make transportation more reliable, e.g. reducing the numbers of traffic jams on any roads. A proper economic climate must also exist as well as other support services. With these factors to influence transportation improvements can become catalysts for economic expansion. However, road transportation improvement that intends to induce job creation, when employers need many lorry drivers to help them to transport products and to move products on the roads often. So, the employers need to employ many transportation workers and lorry drivers to help who to transport their products to send to clients, due to the transportation time is shorten and work efficiency is rasied, so the transportation times are also increasing every day when the road transportation roles are improved. On the other side, improving transportation can raise productivity when many customers need to buy many products and the lorry drivers may drive whose lorries to transport many products between factory and office or between factory to the client's home or between the shop and the client's on the road in the short time fast.

I recommend one model links in an overall road transportation network includes these four modes.

I. Maximizing use of the existing road highway system.

II. Extending or improving the multi-lane divides system local roads and connectors.

III. Continually improving the entire road highway network in response to business activities demand.

The improvement of modern road transportation successful factors include:

● How to improve the highway network

modernization includes obsolete interchanges and other segments of the road, transport network of new designs to improve the life and service of pedestrian walking streets, rebuilding certain in main or minor roads. To the extent that labor markets operate more efficiently and more jobs are created to raise economic expansion if our governments can improve road transportation system to design to satisfy business users demand when lorry drivers need to move or transport whose products on the streets, but who will not influence pedestrian are walking on the streets. Hence, excellent transportation design network can subsequent plan efforts, it can also rise economic efficiency, community and social effects, it can also encourage transportation users to attempt to drive lorries to transport products a lot of times in one day fast and who can also avoid traffic jams occurrence on the road easily. On the one side, economic development is a concept referring to the material aspects of community welfare. There are numerous factors need of development: growth in income and wealth, equitable distribution of income, decreased infant mortality rates, increased literacy rates. On the other side, economic growth means which is sustainable increase in community income and /or wealth. (wealth is the net of resources that generate income). It seems the link between transportation facilities and economic growth has close relationship. Good transportation facilities support economic growth by lowing the transportation costs of users of the transportation network, such as roads. Direct users benefits are reductions in travel, times and fuel consumption, increased reliability and increased safety in the movement of people and products, users' transportation costs are reduced, resources are used for other purpose.

The relationship between transport and economic development occur in two directions, in the sense that (i) land use and economic development are major drivers' of demand for transport (in terms of quantity , type, location and mode); and (ii) transportation investments and other initiatives (such as regulations, pricing) can influence levels, patterns and locations of economic development. The principal role of road transportation is to provide access between spatially separated locations for the business and household sectors, for both commodity (lands transportation) and person movements. For the business sector, this involves connections businesses and their input sources between business factories and other business shops and between business and their markets. For the households sector, it provides people with access to workplaces and education facilities, shops and social recreation, community and medical facilities etc. on the roads. I feel different countries' road transportation system can be self funded in the sense that the majority of the costs of transportation system investment operation and maintenance are either paid directly by users (for example, through car operating costs) are funded initially by governments and recovered from transport users (for example, through petrol duties and road user charges). Governments' road transportation system and their use also give rise to some external costs(externalities). These include global environmental impacts (greenhouse gas emissions) and local environmental and health impacts (for example, noise partial pollution and road accident costs). The direct effects of transportation investments are to reduce road transportation time and costs through reducing travel time, decreasing the operating costs of transportation and enhancing access to destinations within the road network. A good road transportation network also needs to reduce any economic disbenefits, for example where projects reduce congestion or the risk of injury. These incremental benefits of transportation investments may be measured through commercial cost benefit analysis. Other indirect consequences of road transportation network should also be considered when evaluating effects on productivity and the spatial pattern of economic development. Good road transportation design network benefits can include lower costs and enhanced accessibility, due to better transportation links and services expand markets for individual transportation using business and improved access to input.

The economic contribution of road transportation policy can be assessed from various perspectives. These include:

● Effects on aggregate economic welfare (e.g. the sum of consumer and which is the times of cost benefit analysis, as linking to transportation productivity effect.

● Micro economic, for example, enterprise or household level productivity effects.

● Macro economics, for example, contributions to GDP investment or employment and the spatial patterns of economic activity.

One key characteristics of road transportation is split between infrastructure and operations. Infrastructure refers to the right of way on which vehicles operate, which may include ancillary facilities to ensure efficient and effective operations (for example, traffic signals, railway stations). In developed countries, are in most transportation is operated by the private cars, road trucks, the majority of bus and coach services. In long term , overall purpose, to ensure transportation system helps to develop that maximizes the economic and social benefits and minimizes harm. Hence, governments need to concern who are their main target users to use every road. Such as the road is used to near to park and leisure, or local and national economic conditions, keep clean natural environment etc. facilities to provide different benefits to different target users to enjoy to use. It seems that good transportation networks designing can influence economic activities, shopping convenience or business convenience etc. activities to cause whether the country's economic behavior to achieve close relationship successfully. Possible relationship between road networks, location attribute, demand and supply and accessibility and commercial property values of these factors which will influence different countries' concerning to choose where to build main roads and sub minor roads in different cities and rural locations. However, I shall suppose hypotheses how governments to find the most suitable places to build main roads and sub minor roads to whose cities and rural. There is no significant relationship between commercial property values and individual contributions of explanatory variables to variability in commercial property values in whose countries.

In conclusion, I suggest methods how to design suitable transportation networks to governments to build, such as it is essential to establish a technique that may be useful for determining relative accessibility of locations in the network of main roads and sub minor roads. Even, when relative advantages are determined, there is need to develop models that will be useful for predicting commercial properly values. The model may become tool for professional estate surveyors and values to change their practice of using intuition to determine relative access of locations in a road network. Similarly, there is the need to predict the supply of, demand for, and fair market values of commercial properties by developers. Hence if the cities or rural locations can attract many businesses to build commercial properties, governments can build the main roads in the locations. Otherwise, if the cities or rural locations can not attract many businesses to build commercial properties, governments can build the sub minor roads in these locations. Hence, the main roads must have high transportation valuation to let big lorries to drive and park in these main roads easily and conveniently. It seems capital cities may not influence to build the main road factors. Natural environment, commercial properties values, the lands areas size and shape and pedestrian walking numbers on the streets and lorries available numbers on the areas will be other factors to influence where to build main roads in any cities or rural in the country.

In road concept, the route network consists of primary and secondary roads, known as main roads and minor roads respectively. Main roads are usually moderate or high capacity roads that are below highway level of service, carrying large volumes of traffic between areas in urban centers and designed for traffic between neighbors. They have intersections with collector and local streets and commercial areas, such as shopping centers, petrol stations and other businesses are located along such roads. In additions, main roads link up to expressways and freeways with inter-changes in cities or rural. Road network constitutes an important element in urban development , due to urban areas have many farms, gardens, forests , so roads and building needed to provide accessibility required by different land uses and the proper functioning of such urban areas depends an efficient transport network existence. In computing des, the network indicator are used to partition road network into different parts in reasonable way. The results in number of connection to describe density differences in road networks. The parameter records how many roads connect to each road in a network. For two roads with the same length, the ones in the dense area will connect to more roads than that in a sparse area and the connection differences will indicate the density differences to some extent, so road density can also be calculated as the total length of all known roads divided by the total land area in a road divided by the total land area in a road network. Hence, governments need to consider road length to decide how to build main or minor roads to design its transportation systems for businesses activities , such as driving lorries and parking lorries and products are been moving on the streets from roads easily and conveniently. As Wikipedia Contributors (2008) indicate that "transport networks are spatial structures designed to channel flows from the points of demand to points of supply and to link the points together in a transportation system. They are useful for transport network analysis to determine the flow of people, products, services and vehicles." Hence, governments need to research whether where the shopping centers, cinemas, houses, hospitals, schools, offices, factories etc. are located, then, which need to follow these location datas to predict the cars, lorries, taxies, buses etc. of the demand numbers of transportation users to design the lengths, width and distances and the construction of main and minor roads locations and their supply numbers in different capital cities or country roads. It aims to reduce traffic jams and shorten time and air pollution as well as increasing the available spaces to let the lorry drivers to move their logistc on the road easily and reducing the accidents occurrence when the pedestrians are walking on the streets. If the vehicles can be moved on the roads easily. It will also increase time efficiency and productivity to any businessmen. Hence, how to design of the main roads and/or minor roads in any capital or country cities. It will influence any country's economic growth long time in the future.

● Underground train transportation needs to know passenger behaviour reasons

Understanding individual passenger behaviour is essential for the design MTR transportation, because who can choose to catch bus, taxi, tram, train ferry etc. different kinds of public transportation tools. Individual traveler who decides to catch which kinds of public transportation tools, it depends on whether the public transportation tool can provide real time travel information, liking link travel time schedule. So, MTR underground train needs to understand where it has terminal to give convenience to the local living areas of time travelers to choose to catch MTR easily. Although, MTR ticket fare is one factor to influence any passengers choice. But, those other factors can also influence them to choice. e.g. MTR any terminal location of convenience, short time travelling, none crowding in busy (peak) time, MTR platform waiting arrival time, none sudden MTR engineering machines broken accident events occurrence frequently etc. different factors, any one of these factors which can influence passengers who choose to catch MTR or other kinds of transportation tools.

Why route choice can influence passenger behavioural choice ? Usually, the busy time passengers will regard the route choice as a coordination problem to influence them to choose to catch which kinds of transportation tools. The route choice is as an opportunity costs to influence any busy time passengers to decide to choose to catch which kind of transportation tool which is the best right choice in the right time among of them. In the short time, for example, it seems any busy time passengers will choose to catch bus to substitute MTR underground train transportation tool, due to who feels the bus can arrive any destinations to compare other kinds of transportation tools in the most short time. However even if the MTR can either charge cheaper ticket fare to sell full day or charge discount ticket fare to sell in the busy (peak) time to compare to bus fare. It is possible that the busy time passengers will still choose to catch bus, if between the bus terminal and the another bus terminal that distance is the shorter time route to spend time to arrive destination to compare between the MTR terminal to the another MTR terminal arrival time . Also, although the busy time passengers will feel to enounter traffic jam to influence sitting or waiting bus time to be longer time in possible and who also feel MTR can avoid traffic jam problem. However, usually any busy (peak) time passengers will feel the chance of traffic jam occurrence will be less. So, the short bus route choice is more potential factor to influence the busy (peak) time passengers still to choose bus to catch.

However, if anyone wants to investigate results of day-to-day route choice which can be transferred to more realistic environment. It is necessary to explore individual behaviour in an interactive experimental set up to ensure busy (peak) time passenger transportation behavioural choice. For example, a passenger has a choice between a main road (M) and a side road (S) for travelling from (A) to (B). (M) is faster if (M) and (S) are chose by the same number of passengers. So, this method can be researched whether MTR terminal station is located at the main road (M) or the side road (S) where is more suitable to accept to passengers generally.

Why trip time reliability and crowding factors can influence MTR passenger choice? Other problem is MTR busy (peak) time's crowding in public transportation occurrence of MTR underground train transportation tool is becoming a growth to concern as MTR demand growth at a busy (peak) time. To capture the MTR passengers benefits with reduced crowding from improved MTR public transport service and image. It is necessary a identify the relevant dimensions of crowding that are meaningful measures of what crowding means to MTR passengers. Two main influences on MTR model choice that are growing in relevance are trip time reliability and crowding. It represents a benefit-cost framework. In fact, MTR passengers can be willing to pay more expensive ticket fare, it MTR can avoid crowding and short and the accurate arrival trip time between terminals is reliable to occur. How to measure of MTR crowding, e.g. weighting the gap between the busy time, the standard (i.e. objective) and the perceived (i.e. subjective) metrics. We are not in a position to definitely map the two dimensions, which is a crucial requirement for translating objective improvements into equivalent subjective gains that then can be applied, willingness to pay estimates MTR ticket fares to obtain the additional MTR passenger benefits of MTR public transportation investment to any terminal stations. Because MTR crowding has a negative impact on passengers in terms of psychological on emotional distress. MTR passengers are willing to stand for up to 20 minutes of the service is fast and reliable. However crowding outweighed these benefits from a MTR passenger's perpective, experienced crowding leads a increased dissatisfaction. e.g. stress and less privacy during who needs to stand up in MTR. Due to there are no enough places to supply to them to stand up in MTR. If the MTR trip time was longer time between the passenger's terminals, who will feel more dissatisfaction and it will cause who feels whether who ought need to choose to catch other transportation tools to substitute MTR next time. e.g. bus, train, tram, ferry, taxi etc. So, from an operator's perspective, the MTR service frequency or MTR size is significantly influenced by the level of ridership, which sends a signal to respond if the monitored crowding level exceeds the benchmark standard in the busy time. e.g. in the morning time or at the night time, the students or employment people who need to go to schools or offices (working places). The locations of different places between MTR terminals and crowding are regarded as a key service attribute for MTR pubic transportation along with other factors, such as travelling time and reliability, e.g. service quality, none engineering machines are broken to cause MTR stops suddenly.

Given the increasing importance of crowding on both the disutility to existing MTR public transportation users and the influence to it. MTR passenger can choose to use either the MTR public public transportation or other public transportation. It is timely to review the MTR current measures of crowding defined by transportation authorities. MTR operators ought evaluate whether they apporpriately reflect MTR each traveler experiences and perceptions of crowding in busy (peak) time. I suggest that MTR needs to buy other underground trains to supply to the busy (peak) time passengers to let them have enough seats to sit down, so who do not need to stand up in any MTR underground trains when they catch MTR underground trains in busy time. It aims to let who are willingness to pay the estimation of reasonable ticket fares to compare the other kinds of transportation tools in the busy (peak) time.

What is the crowding difference between train and MTR underground train? In fact, crowding won't be happened to brother these transportation tools easily in the busy time and non busy time both. e.g. bus, taxi, train, tram, ferry. Because passengers can not choose to stand up in these transportation tools easily, due to these transportation tools have no enough areas (spaces) to let them to stand up easily . So, the crowding will be avoided to occur in these tranportation tools usually. Otherwise, MTR will have many passengers who can choose to stand up because MTR design of length is very long and it has enough areas (places) to let passengers to choose to stand up, even there have none any seats are provided to let them to sit down. So, MTR passengers will feel more dissatisfaction and crowding easily, especial in any peak (busy) time every day.

Comparing to bus, much more diverse crowding measures are defined in the passenger rail industry. For passenger, different specifications for measuring crowding are found across countries and even within a country. For example, rail crowding measures in the UK, the passengers in excess of capacity is crowding measure that applies to all London and South east operators weekday train services at a London terminus during the morning peak from 0700 to 09: 59 , and those departing during the afternoon peak from 16:00 to 18:59 (office of rail regulation 2011 year). The overall PIXC figure is considered the planned standard class capacity of each train service as well as the actual number of standard class passengers on the service at the critical point. i.e. the location on a trains of standard class passengers that surpass the planned capacity as the difference between the number of actual passengers and the capacity of the train divided by the number of passenger is within the capacity . So, it seems train and MTR underground public transportaton tools had been encountering the crowding problems in peak time, the difference in train passengers need to wait next train or more train arrival is who doesn't plan to enter the train, when who discovers the current train has no seats to provide to them to sit down in whose trip. Otherwise, MTR passengers can choose either to stand up within the large areas (places) if who discovered there are no any seats to provide to them to sit down or who can wait the next MTR arrival in order to who can sit down. It seems MTR transportation tool crowding environment includes in waiting platform and inside of the MTR underground train. Otherwise, train transportation tool crowding environment only includes the waiting platform and the passengers will not have crowding feeling inside of the train, due to none of passengers choose to stand up inside any trains because any train inside has no enough places to let them to stand up. How MTR can attract many passengers. On the commuter departure time choice of any reference point researching hand, the departure time decisions of commuters are of fundamental importance of peak period MTR traffic congestion. However, whether on the demand side, MTR underground train congestion relief measures, such as MTR ticket fare to every terminal station needs to be charged cheaper fare or discount fare in the peak (busy) time every day. To aim to attract many passengers to choose to catch MTR Underground train public transportation tools, substitute to choose other public transportation tools in the peak time.

Over the past decades, there have been very active research efforts in the departure time problem, both in econometric modeling and dynamic user equilibrium fields. Although, these works provide valuable insights into dynamic commuter decision making, they do not identify the commuters' response to gains and losses related to whole actual arrival time to reference points who may have relative. The appliability of the reference point hypothesis of prospect theory to the commuter's departure time decision making to obtain a better understanding of how departure time choice in MTR platform during their waiting underground train arrival time. However, every MTR underground train actual arrival time and deviation variables related to reference points (gains and losses) are the key factors in the departure time choice model. How the MTR underground train of every communter's daily departure time decision can be modelled when the reference point hypothesis of prospect theory. The MTR underground train's schedule delay is defined as the difference between the preferred arrival time (PAT) and the actual arrival time (AT) for a given MTR communter. In a daily MTR commute, a commuter in the indifference band actual arrival time is an essential feature of MTR schedule study. Two reference points are the earliest acceptable arrival time and the work starting time for a given MTR platform waiting passengers. In psychological view point, prospect theory proposes that the displeasure of a loss is perceived or greater than the pleasure of a gain of the same attitude and therefore, the value function is stronger for losses than gains.

To conclude, it seems that if MTR waiting passengers need not spend long time to wait underground train arrival in platform and it can provide seats to let them to sit down in the busy (peak) crowding time. It will make them to feel pleasure, even the MTR ticket fare is not fair and reasonable to charge higher fare to compare other kinds of public transportation tools fares. So the peak waiting time factor can influence the passengers to choose other kind of transportation tools to catch easily. Moreover, MTR's two reference points are the earliest role. Similarly a loss is observed when the MTR platform waiting commuter experiences or actual arrival time which is beyond that the MTR schedule time. Due to that a MTR waiting commuter is as an early side arrival of whose actual arrival time is earlier than whose preferred arrival time.

Reference
Bailey, L., Mokhtarian, P.L. Little, A. (2008). The broader Connection Between Public Transportation, Energy Conservation And Greenhouse Gas Reduction, Report Prepared As Part Of TCRP Project J-11/Tasks Transit Cooperative Research Program, Transportation Research Board Submitted To American Public Transportation Association in http://www.apta.com/research/into/online/land_use.cfmi, accessed 17 April 2008.

The UK Standing Advisory Committee On Trunk Road Assessment (SACTRA) (1999). Transport And The Economy (Report To UK DETR). Retrieved From: http://webarchive.nationalarchives.gov.uk/20050301192906 ;   http://dft.gov.uk/stellent/groups/dft-econappr/documents/pdf/dft_econappr_pdf_022512.pdf

Wikipedia Contributors (2008). Arterial Roads In Wikipedia, The Free Encyclopeda,   http://en.wikipedia.org/w/index.php?title=Arterial_road&oldid=212832640(accessed May30,2008).

● How to let passengers feel impact of undergrouund train transport to their
working time efficiency

Any countries must need road, sea and air transport to assist businessmen to transport products in local or overseas. If the country's road , sea or air transport system service quality is poor. It will influence any products transport time, speed, inefficient transport to anywhere.
How to raise the country's transport system in order to improve efficiencies to let any businessmen can deliver their products to anywhere easily,e.g. warehouses, client homes, supermarkets destination in the most short time to avoid delay occurrence to let clients feel unsatisfactory or complaint their perform their delivery services poorly. I shall discuss the factors how to improve any countrues' transport systems to achieve the most efficient way as below:

Any countries' transport systems will create economic value, e.g. demonstrate value for money, economic worth, viable commercial worth, financial affordable worth, achieveable worth. Any countries' transport systems can bring welfare value by economics. It has direct relationship to take the form of measured economic activity, i.e. GDP. The form of measured economic activity can impact on any countries' economic economic geography, locally , regionally and nationally's local GDP impacts. The welfare impacts may include: leisure time savings, e.g. the local people drive cars or catch any public transportation tools to go to any geogrpahical location's shopping centers, big gardens, swimming pools, cinemas etc. places to carry on any kinds of leisure activities.

Environmental impacts may include avoiding noise, air pollution on road transportation aspect , when the main road is only on on focus on the main city,

but the city lacks other roads to let any drivers can choose them to drive, instead of the main road in the city. Then, when many cars are driven on the busy transport

time, e.g. morning working time or night busy time between 6:00 and 9:00 AM, between 6:00 and 9:00 PM. When either many working people need to catch public transport or drive themselves cars to go to offices to work or they need to catch pubic transport tools or drive themselves cars to home. Then, the only one main road problem will need them to stay themselves cars on roads, due to traffic jam or traffic accidence occurrence problem causes when many cars are driven on the road in the busy transport time. It will influence they can not go to offices or homes easily daily, even in the busy transport time, their cars' gas need to be used much to cause air pollution and traffic noise is easily caused easily in the busy transport time on the road. When the city has only one main road for drivers in the busy transport time. So, poor road transport system can bring poor impact on economic welfare benefits arising from proved labour supply from commuting, time savings, including exchequer benefits. Consequently, the county's GDP will be fallen down, due to labour market effects which do not add to welfare value.

Whether can poor transport system impact indirectly on GDP or not on local, regional , or national economic geography impacts? Does transport lead to greater economic activity i.e. higher GDP? DO they lead to change in economic activity location? Does transport impact the existence of business location and new economic activity opportunities? The measurement on every country's transport how impacts on economic change, facilitating geographic division of labour and specialization. It can be analyzed on these general aspects:

Costs and speed of travel time (Economic value of travel time savings) . Travel time savings to users from improved transport is a key of economic value, but it has only less influence,journey time reliability is more important to business frieght as well as business travellers, network connectivity enhancements as well as business travellers, network connectivity enhancement can help people and goods travel more quickly (i.e. linked to jounrey time and journey time reliability, as well as opening new destinations and new journeys, comfort and quality service provision is relevant to public transport, e.g. detering jounreys at particular times or by certain modes (e.g. overcrowding), impact on productivity at work for commuters, safety and security , due to loss of output from workers, transport accidents occur easily. All of these issues will impact any countries' standard of living to local people (geography) , even GDP income.

Why does the direct and indirect effects of transportation have a positive impact on the economic growth and development of a country? Does it influence acccess to goods, services and

employment opportunities in any regions? Underdeveloped countries must need to consider how transport system influences their economic growth. For example, the costs of transportation and production are reduced through timely delivery and enhancing the economies of scale in the production process, when the road is often traffic joam, gas cost, time waste , air pollution cost, noise has many roads, but if one lorry drivers needs drive more than one day to day to deliver goods to another city's warehouse every day. It will bring psychological pressure in terrible, when they need long time to drive on the road. They can not sleep easily because road accident will occur easily when they need to spend long time to drive lorries on the road.

So, how to solve the long driving time on road transport problem will be one issue concerns human life welfare benefit aspect, instead of economic benefit aspect. The transport system welfare worth needs to include human life worth. It is a valuable insight into the causality (ot lack of causality) between transport and economic growth and will serve to compare to any countries' national level and local geographical disocation level both.

In special, underdeveloped countries' public transport time whether it is long or short factor, it will influence workers their going to offices to work time. If they often need spend long time to catch buses, due to traffic jam,then it will influence their efficiences to be reduced, productive number is influenced to reduce also, because traffic jam causes they often go to offices too lately.It can influence workers' bad emotion to work every day. So, traffic jam will bring negative relationship between low efficiency and bad emotion to the workers, because they need to spend long time to wait, public transportation tools and traffic jam also influence their working emotion. Consequently, service and working performance will be influenced to poor, because long time traffic jam problem causes their bad emotion to work. It is one critical factor in the path of more widely spread economic growth and urbanization for traffic jam problem to underdeveloped countries.

However, transport system can also influence developed countries' economy. How does it influence on environmental impacts aspect from mature stage. Its business activities must raise, dramastic expansion during this period, such as underdeveloped country, US, UK. In order to acheive long term sustainable development , new demands are being placed on transport sector, such as underground mass transit rail transport , ferry, local air frieght transport, train , e.g. Japan, Fance, US high speed prior rail. Because their developed countries , business and entertainment activities needs increase, it influences high time efficient and rapid speed public transportation tools needs are also needed in societies. These new technological public transport tools invention will impact on climate, noise, human health, land use and damage to ozene layer, acidification aspects, instead of economic beneficial aspect.

For long -term sustainable development to be achieved, the various activities within developed and underdeveloped societies must be adapted to what can be tolerated by humans and by the natural environment. Transport is an activity which affects humans and the natural environment for both the development of society as a whole as well as for the mobility for the individual. For Swedish underdeveloped country example, air pollution in Swedish urban areas has beed reduced, but in many places concentrations of certain substances deiving from transport activities are still at unacceptable levels and much more has to be done. Carbon dioxide emissions and noise are examples of environmental problems demanding further efforts. Measures to limit the exploitation of valuable natural and cultural environments to protect biological diviersity are also needed. So, if Swedish still hopes to develop its tourism industry to attract many travellers to choose to travel itself country. It needs to solve environmental problems from different modes of transport are of different dimensions, such as improving its air transport to avoid cause different problems and rail transport differs in turn from road transport.

The transport problem to Swedish may include poor technological communication information to its public and purchasers of transportation and communication services as to the environmental effects of different solutions is significant in creating the demand for environmentally sound public transport service concepts. It is therefore important that such lacking high technological communication and information system is presented in as completem accurate and clear way as a method for non-monetary comparison of the environmental public transport service system aspect.

In real, it's public tranport service system is needed to be improved and upgraded in order to let travellers feel Swedish's any rail, underground train, ferry, bus , taxi etc. different public transport travelling service can provide excellent performance to serve their travelling passengers, when they need to catch any kinds of public transport tools to go to travel. They can feel convenient and comfortable to attract them to visit Swedish to travel again. Then, its tourism industry GDP income will be raised, if Swedish government can innovate any new kinds of purchase ticket equipment to install in and public transport stations to let travelling passengers feel that they do not need to spend long time to queue to buy tickets to catch ferry, train, underground mass transit rail on stations conveniently. Because long time purchase ticket queue waiting will cause travellers feel its public service performance dissatisfaction and they will complain , even they won't choose to catch the kind of public transport, even the travellers won't choose to travel Swedish again, if they feel Swedish is one developed country, but it neglects to take care about travellers' catching public transport travelling service needs.

It is one poor or bad feeing to let travellers choose to Swedish again. Hence, Swedish needs to improve its public transport service performance in order to achieve to raise their comfortable and satisfactory catching public transport tools needs to let travellers to feel. They may include efficient land use for transportation tools, comprising issues concerning natural and cultural environment, natural resources, biological diversity and aesthetics, noise reducing, public transportation energy consumption and time consumption reducing, raising public transport service facilities performance functions and other issues concerning the model. For example, Swedish government can facilitate the public transport price conparison and journey time spending comparison information gathering enquiring machines public transportation selection method of public transportation services to let every travellers can evaluate different modes of public transport when they are staying in ferry, bus, train, underground mass transit rail, taxi stations.

A travelling family can seek its sustainable transport selection system for passenger transport tool. When they touch the enquiry machine, they can compare busm ferry, train, underground train, taxi price and journey spending time from their transportation stations to another destinations. Then, travelling passengers can compare these public transport tools ticket prices, journey spending time immediately when they touch the public transport enquiring machines in stations any time. Then, they can make the most righ choice to decide whether they ought catch which kind of public transport tool to arrive the another journey destination. It is one every attractive high technological enquiry method to help any travelling passegners to choose which kind of public transport tool, it can be the most cheap transport tool at the moment in any public transport stations. So , for developed countries innovative its public transport service performance will need future passengers' journey needs daily. Hence, they can not neglect how to improve public transport service needs to satisfy passengers to feel satisfaction, if Sweden government hopes its tourism industry can raise GDP income in long time.

● How underground train MTR can let passengers to feel catching time reducing

It has close relationship between globalization and global tranport development. How globalisation impacts on the environment via changes taking place in the transport sectors. In fact, it is not clear how the relative price changes that result from openness will affect the environental composition of economic activity. For example, some countries will produce more environmentally intensive goods, others will produce fewer. On the other hand, liberalisation will raise incomes, perhaps increasing the willingness to pay for environmental improvement. These potential income effects increased outweigh the negative scale effects with increased economic activities. When combined with the positive effects with technology transfer, the net effect on local pollutants could be positive . Hence, we need to find methods to solve the problem of raising transport economic activities and serious environmental pollution creating as the same time occurrence.

Globalisation helps to facilitate greater division of labor, and to exploit its comparative advantage more completely. In longer term, globalization also stimilates technology an dlabour transfers, and allows the dynamism that accompanies economic activities to stimulate the development of new transport technologies and short time transport processes that lead to global welfare improvement.

On shipping transport industry aspect, shipping will increase ocean pollution, when international shipping activities are increasing. Trade and shipping encourages energy use in shipping is coupled with the movement of waterborne commerce. The estimates depending on the transport goods number of at-sea or in port days much increase globally every day. The energy demand of international shipping fuel sale number and domestically assigned fuel sales number also increases for global fuel usage. Estimates of ocean going ships now consume about 2% to 3% and perhaps even as much as 4% of world fossil fuels.Hence, when global shipping energy fuel usage number increases, because global shipping trading activities number increases. It will bring the environmental pollution to ocean level increases. On air transport industry aspect, their travellers' catching air plans travelling needs and businesses' goods transport air delivery service needs are increasing from the requirements for high quality , fast and reliable international transport. Moreover, the networks that airline companies operate have changed often to hub-and spoke networks, many new often low -cost companies have entered the air freight market, any long time air journey is needed, e.g. Australia airline expands its one new air journey flies to UK, it needs two days flying time. It means that every flight to UK from Australia , it needs to use more fuel to fly. Then , air pollution will increase also.

On road transport industry aspect, global road transport cost and transit times, traffic jam occurrence chances also increase because when the road building number is increasing globally. So, it will cause traffic jam and long journey time spending , even fuel usage spending number is also increased. Then, accident occurrence chance is raised. Hence, global business or entertainment transport activities number increasing , it will bring much negative impact on environmental pollution, traffic jams number increases, long journey spending time increases, fuel usage number increases. Although , frequent transport activities may bring GDP income.

On transport service industy aspect, but is also brings negative influence to standard of living. It means that when transport fuel demand increases, transport activities number increases, GDP income on relative any transport activities needs industy , e.g. logistic demand needs, when lorry drivers need to drive lorries to deliver goods from one warehouse to another warehouse or supermarket or office etc. different business places on the road driving activities increase. But, it also bring air pollution , traffic noise and traffic jam etc. transport problems to road and natural environment and raises worse standard of living , bad emotion to working people or learning emotion to students , due to frequent traffic jam causes , low efficiency and productivity to workers, even student individual learning time can be reduced if they need to spend long time to wait bus, ferry, rail, underground train to go to schools , due to frequent long time traffic jam occurs on the roads to influence they can not go to schools on time often when they are catching buses to go to schools absolutely in busy transport time.

Thus, although any countries need to consider how to design their transport system, e.g. how to e.g. how to choose the right locations to build roads to let many cars can be driven available easily when the morning and evening (office and school transport busy time, e.g. 6:00 to 9:00 AM morning, 6:00 to 9:00 PM in the evening transport time usually because these two transport periods are usually , there are many students and working people need to catch any public transportation or drive cars tools to go back homes. So, enough roads number and long and not narrow road area must be needed to design in order to let enough cars be driven on the roads in the transport busy times to the countries have many big cities or have high population , such as UK, US, China, India, Hong Kong. They have many people , but drivers and cars numbers both are increasing. So, efficient road design and road number are also needed to increase in order to let drivers can transport goods to deliver, students and working people can catch any public transport tools to arrive any destinations on reads in the short time rapidly in order to avoid to spend long time transportation time and late to arrive any destinations in possible occurrence. So, any sudden traffic jam is not hoped to be caused by easy traffic accidents occurrence any time.

Hence, global efficient road transport system is needed, when global transport activities are increased, because any road logistic transport activities are increasing, they will also influence the students and working people when they also need to catch any public transport tools or drive themselves cars to go to working places or schools on the roads at the same busy transport time between 6:00 to 9:00 AM morning busy transport time and between 6:00 to 9:00 PM evening busy transport time. Because these both times will be have many students, working people , they need either go to offices or schools or go to homes. Hence, if the country had many lorry drivers need to drive their lorries to deliver goods on the roads in the transport busy morning or evening time in the same driving time on the roads. It will increase the risk to cause frequent traffic jam or traffic accident occurrence easily in possible in the country. So, any countries' governments can not neglect how to design roads and choose anywhere are the roads suitable locations to be built as well as anywhere land useful number to build road location choices in order to solve geographical traffic jams occurrence chance.

Hence, globalization of transport activities may bring geographical GDP growth, but it also bring traffic jams and traffic accidents occurrences, hearing impairment due to traffic noise, air pollution, traffic crashed, bad working emotions to workers and bad learning emotions to students, due to spending long transport time when traffic jam or traffic accidence occurs more easily.

However, transportation is an important tool if a country's progress. Rapid economic growth and increasing level of urbanization enhances a person's living standard have, it leads to a greater travel demands. Hence, governments ought not neglect have to design its roads , measure every road's length or width whether it has how many cars need to drive in morning or evening transport busy time for students, working people and delivery goods drivers of public transportation tools or private transportation tools easy driving needs in order to avoid frequent traffic jams or traffic accidents occurrences in possible.

Moreover, any governments also need to solve these issues, if they hope to develop their transport system successfully. These issues include : What mode of transportation to cost-effective in meeting a region's transportation needs to the country? How should a state department of transportation prioritize its highway delivers to maximize economic growth? What is the trade-off between additional growth in urban area and the cost of expanding transportation systems to accommodate greater growth? What effect does the expansion of transportation systems have on the need to invest in other types of transport modes? For example , the transport expansion may include the construction of additional highway segments, rail lines, runways, or additional sea, air, rail or bus terminal capacity using traditional technology; highway may include the additional of lanes to an interstate highway system; the conversion of an existing two-lane road to a four lane limited access highway, replacement or widening of bridges, and the extension of an existing road. Airport examples, include runway lengthening, apron expansion, and additional terminal gates.

On the other hand, enhancement to new transport technologies may bring efficiency of the existing highway system, examples may include intelligent highway systems, congestion pricing, intermodal freight facilities, geographic positioning systems, and instrument landing systems to mention of a few major transport innovations. So, transport policy makers need to understand the effects of these new transport mode innovations on economic development or GDP growth on transport activities growth transportation services and a more efficient use of limited land supplying scarce resources , air quality ,and noise pollution, traffic jams, long spending transport time to students, working people, entertaining people, even deliver goods lorry drivers their every day essential driving activities or catching public transportation tools needs problems. For example, the concept of intelligent highway systems needs increase trend. In simply , vehicles are being linked to each other and to traffic control devices to improve the efficiency of the total highway system. Similar types of innovations in intelligent traffic management are increasing needs for air, sea, and rail systems. The question is that whether intelligent highway systems can attribute of highways on economic development, raising on productivity of reducing highway congestion or improving pavement condition.

In fact, many developed countries' transportation system is mature. The nation has gone beyond the frontier of building, the interstate highway system and connecting most cities (markets). Tweaking the system with additional lanes and the new intelligent highway systems are useful in China, US, UK, because they have many cities. SO, road efficient traffic congestion control is needed when many students, working people, delivery goods transport people need to drive cars or catch cars on every city's roads in the transport busy time between 6:00 to 9:00 AM morning transport busy time as well as between 6:00 to 9:00 PM evening transport busy time.

However, transportation investment must be needed, if the country hoped to have good economic productivity, efficient transport service can bring good effects on the flows goods and people on roads every day when they use the country's transport system. So, any countries need to collect data, they can not be lack of enough transport information in any time that links anywhere locations of any drivers to the locations of the transport system that provide them with services in any time, e.g. every day morning and evening transport busy time, radio can report the real transport time of any roads traffic jam or traffic accident message to let drivers to listen to know whether anywhere roads are occurring traffic accidents or traffic jams or when the road traffic accident or traffic jam is solved to let the drivers can know whether when the roads can be opened to drive again. So, real time road transport message information is needed to report by radio, in order to let any drivers to know whether they ought choose to drive themselves cars on the road when they need to choose anywhere road to drive to the destination if they can know when the road has traffic accident or traffic jam occurs. They won't drive their cars on the road in the moment immediately.

On conclusion, globalization can being frequent transport economic activities. So, road , air, sea, transport service users' transport service needs are also increased. Every country ought not neglect how to innovate their transport service in order to satisfy their transport needs to achieve economic growth, efficient and short transport time spending, productivities increase, reducing air pollution, traffic noise , raisins standard of living on transport influence aspect to satisfy working people, students, entertaining people, delivery goods transport users' efficient road transport time behavioral spending aspect.

Artificial Intelligent In Road Transportation Strategy
● How artificial intelligent vehicle may interact intelligent transportation tools

Can artificial intelligence (AI) and machine learning (ML) be used in the search for new " consumption" behavioral type variables that affect consumer individual or transportation service organization individual different transportation tools choices, such as road or sea or sky transportation tools? Can artificial intelligent vehicle may interact intelligent transportation tools market development?
Consumers usually have bargaining and on risk choice when they are already shopping, such as who need to accept to use any (AI) new technological products to replace human traditional behaviors, such as intelligent non-manual driving transportation market, e.g. cars are needed to be driven by human drivers on road, but it has bargaining and on risky choice, when non-manual (AI) vehicle buyers who need to depend on non-manual artificial intelligent (ML) system assists them to drive their cars on the roads.

So, any non-manual driving auto car buyers must need to believe (AI) non-manual driving vehicles (ML) systems can make accurate driving judgement to reduce or avoid any traffic accident occurrences more than human drivers' driving judgement when the (ML) systems are driving their cars on the roads. Then the intelligent vehicle manufacturers will have possible to sell their non-manual driving vehicles success.

This is the first reason or idea influences consumer individual choice to buy any kinds of (AI) non-manual driving vehicles, when consumers believe (ML) systems are more safe and make more accurate judgement to compare human or computer systems, when they are sitting in one non-manual auto driving vehicle on the road.

The another second reason or idea is that some common limits on driving consumer prediction might be understood as the kinds of errors made by poor implementation of machine learning.

Supposing driving consumers believe (AI) machine learning ability is worse to compare to human learning ability. It will also influence driving consumers do not accept to use any (AI) non-manual auto driving vehicles to replace every driver is essential on driving by himself/herself on the road. The third idea or reason is that it is important to influence driving customers believe how (AI) non-manual auto driving technology is used in them can both overcome and exploit human driving skill and safe limits and raise more auto driving safe judgement to compare human driving safe judgement.

However, how to predict any kinds of (AI) non-manual driving vehicles future consumption effort, due to different kinds of (AI) non-manual driving transportation vehicles which have different unique functions and designs to be used by different kinds of road transportation or driving demand of consumers. For example, lorry drivers need non-manual intelligent system can help them to drive fast, but safe to assist them to transport cargo to arrive destinations from their factories or offices. Otherwise, private car driver expects whose (AI) non-manual driving vehicle can auto drive to send to whom to arrive destination in safe way and non-too fast and non-too slow speed in order to avoid accident occurrences.

So, a different road intelligent consumer demand is to define whose individual driving behavior and driving habit and driving attitude and driving judgement and driving speed demand to decide how to design whose intelligent vehicle to satisfy those driving demand more generally, as simply being open-minded about what variables are likely to influence every consumer economic choice, when who decide either to buy any kinds of (AI) products or not to buy any kinds of (AI) products to replace the different demand of consumers their different (AI) useful demand.

Hence, for these three (AI) products group of stakeholders, such as home (AI) consumer group, firm (AI) consumer group and government (AI) consumer group . These consumer groups may consider whether different kinds of (AI) products can give what is special beneficial interest to them to use. These variables can be measurable properties of choices to influence them to choose to buy any (AI) kinds of (AI) products to use, e.g. psychophysiological, biological, social influences, consumer's wealth, moods and personality, (AI) product price etc. variable factors which will influence them to decide to attempt to buy any kinds of (AI) products to use. If behavioral economics is as open-mindedness about what variables might predict. Then , (AI) machine learning system is a way to do behavioral economics because it can make use of a wide set of variables and select-which ones predict.

In behavioral economic view point, when general consumer overall demand to the product is much than the other similar (AI) non auto driving vehicle products, such as any kinds of (AI) non-manual auto driving vehicles and any kinds of manual driving vehicles case, then any kinds of (AI) non-manual auto driving vehicles will be more attractive to cause many manual driving vehicle buyers choose to buy (AI) non-manual auto driving vehicles. Hence, it seems if any kinds of (AI) non-manual auto driving vehicle products can make more attractive variable efforts to influence overall driving consumers to feel that they have more needs to drive non-manual auto vehicles to compare more than driving manual driving vehicle.

What is the main variable effort to intelligent vehicles to attract driving consumers to choose to accept to drive them ? However, I believe that (AI) machine learning system is a main factor to raise overall driving consumers' acceptances to drive it to replace manual driving vehicle. If it can persuade or prove (AI) machine learning system ability and judgement effort is more accurate than human or computer learning effort or judgement effort, then it is possible that any kinds of (AI) non-manual driving vehicle products will be accepted to drive on the road in popular.

Machine learning system is able to find prediction value in details of how the bargaining occurs. This discovery is the beginning of the next step for driving consumer individual driving behaviors or driving habits. It raises questions that include: What variables predict to influence driving consumers to change whose driving habits or driving attitudes? How can driving consumer individual emotion, face-to-face talking with whose friends when they are sitting in the non-manual driving vehicle to influence whom driving habit or driving attitude to be changed ? Do driving consumers consciously understand why those habit driving attitudes variables are important when they are sitting in one intelligent vehicle? Can (AI) driving machine learning methods capture the effects of motivated cognition to influence driving consumers decide to buy any kinds of (AI) non-manual auto vehicle products more attractively. So, it seems (AI) driving machine learning method is a main variable factor to influence driving consumers to feel who have more confidence to drive them more than any other kinds of similar manual driving vehicles on the road.

Consequently, (AI) driving machine learning system will be one important psychological method to influence driving consumers to choose to buy (AI) auto driving vehicle products to replace manual driving vehicles. The reason is because human and driving machine learning system both which will have limited variable factors to influence general different countries (AI) driving consumers' need desire to be raised.

● Why can (AI) driving machine learning system main factor influence driving consumer individual desires ?

Driving consumer expectations are hard to measure or predict driving attitudes and driving behaviors in (AI) non-manual driving vehicles market. Artificial intelligence is another kind of computer science development to apply intelligent vehicle market. Why do driving consumers feel need to buy any kinds of (AI) auto driving vehicles to drive to replace manual driving vehicles on the roads? What are (AI) auto driving features different to manual driving features?

(AI) is the recreation of cognitive functions in computers; it enables machines to perform tasks like humans and perhaps even better than human. In the real world, scientists develop the technological singularity, in which a superintelligence emerges with unfold human consequences.

Professionals in many industries are intensely interested in the specifics of what (AI) can do today, and how can it helps. They are considering the impact of applied (AI), in which computers are used to address a particular problem, extracting and utilizing patterns found in large volumes of data. Of all (AI)'s subfields, machine learning is attracting the most attention. I shall explain why (AI) machine learning system is the main factor to lead consumers feel need to buy any (AI) products to use. Such as below:

For smartphone, fraud detection to medical diagnosis etc. applied (AI) technological products examples. (AI) machine learning systems can help any one of these products to do any exceed general computer learning systems which (AI) learning systems can do any skills to supply (AI) users to use to compare computer learning systems can not do any skills to supply compute users to use. It seems that (AI) machine learning system is the unique feature to attract consumer consideration in technological product market.

An term for different types of learning, and can be accomplished using different techniques. This has led to a perception that all marketing teams should have (AI) to bring a unified personalized customer experience, when consumers choose to buy any (AI) products to feel what are the different or unique characteristics to compare general computer products. Such as (AI) product has this unique machine learning characteristics, we can predict (AI) and machine learning is connected to influence consumers to feel needs.

Furthermore, over the same time period, and in contrast to predictions for roles in many industries. (AI) won't take the place of marketers and merchandisers themselves although it is already a new value to analytical and strategic marketing skills to persuade consumers to buy any (AI) products. It means different kinds of (AI) products will have different machine learning effort and unique characteristics to attract consumers to choose to buy them to use. Such as, when intelligent vehicles need have unique road driving or sea transportation or flying machine learning system when they are applied on these three kinds of transportation tool aspects. They need have good response safety driving and immediate response learning systems to avoid any boats or air planes or vehicles to crash to them to reduce accident occurrences immediately on any one of either road or sky or sea journey environment.

What is the reason why (AI) driving machine learning system can influence good at making sense to driving consumer desire? Only humans (drivers) , preferably experienced, well informed humans can understand their driving customer needs and decide how to design or reengineer any (AI) intelligent vehicle product functions. (AI) intelligent vehicle can give these professionals the means to do this better to compare manual driving immediate response control function when any vehicles are driving or they will stop immediately to close / near to them in order to reduce crash occurrence on the road, and then maximize relevance through real-time customization of the non-manual auto vehicle driving user experience.

For example, as ever, senior decision makers need to be informed, decisive and results-oriented or risk losing out. Harvard Business Review indicated : Over the next decade, (AI) won't replace managers, but managers who use (AI) will replace those who don't. Such as intelligent vehicle won't replace drivers, but drivers who use intelligent vehicles will replace those who can not control how to drive their vehicles in the most safe way. So, (AI) driving machine learning system will have possible to do any drivers' (human's) driving judgement, driving analytical mind and driving effort to be more accurate than manual driving skills. Such as how to control to drive the intelligent vehicle in the most safe way. It is general manual driving skill can not achieve to drive in the safe way.

For another (AI) digital commerce example, (AI) and machine learning are the most exciting developments in marketing and merchandising to be applied to digital commerce, such as making better decisions through trend and cluster analysis, deploying product and content in mutually reinforcing combinations, increasing customer engagement and satisfaction in real time.

Hence, the key attraction in digital commerce circles is that machine learning is designed to be self-optimizing. Optimizing for revenue example will surface are increasingly profitably selection of products (within the brand parameters selected).

When to apply (AI) capabilities and what value (AI) is delivering for customer and company like. Unlike any technology before it, (AI) is analytical and predictive capabilities offers the prospect for each and every individual. It can maximize real time and engagement. Effective tailored (AI) technology, such as digital experience cloud technology is available now. And once integrated, (AI) starts learning and delivering incremental value from day one. So (AI) could transform the digital experience to any business organizations.

Hence, (AI) driving machine learning system can be applied to road driving skill aspect. When intelligent vehicles are invented to own the most safe driving judgement skill and they can know when either they may auto drive fast speed, when they are feeling to know when there are not many vehicles are moving close/near to them or when they need auto drive slow speed, when they are feeling to know when there are many vehicles are moving close/ near to them. Then driving consumers will have more confidence to choose to buy any kinds of intelligent vehicles to replace manual driving vehicles to drive on the roads.

● Non-manual driving transportation tool market development

If Non-manual driving vehicle manufacturers expect their (AI) automatic vehicles can attract drivers to buy. I feel them to need to consider how (AI) driving machine learning system can achieve these requirements in order to satisfy manual driving vehicle drivers' requirement to change their traditional driving habit to choose non-manual driving needs. It means (AI) driving machine learning systems can help them to drive vehicles to replace manual driving vehicles on the road. This is the main factor to influence car buyers choose to buy intelligence driving vehicles replace to manual driving vehicles. I believe (AI) non-manual driving vehicle machine learning systems, need to be designed as below:

(1) Improving driving safety by preventing accidents from happening.

Every year, drivers are facing a large number of casualties, due to traffic accidents. The amount of killed and injured road traffic related accidents is increasing every year. The real cost of an accident can go well beyond the limits of immediate material destruction, and is impossible to evaluate.

Hence, researchers and car manufacturers are looking for solutions in order to reduce the amount of accidents. They already developed a considerable set of technologies in order to decrease the amount of casualties. Most of them (like airbags, seat-belts, anti-lock systems, shock absorbing car bodies) are efficient in decreasing the impact of an accident, and in protecting the passengers of the cars. The technologies already saved a lot of lives, but they are rarely able to avoid accidents because they do not anticipate them. Moreover, if they are protecting in many cases, the passengers of the car, they do not prevent most traffic participants, like pedestrians on bicyclists from getting injured. it causes (AI) non-manual automatic car manufacturers need to consider how to design machine learning safety system is to prevent accident from happening instead of just reducing their impact.

This can only be possible using intelligent systems that can observe the driving environment, reason and decide if there is a danger, determine how to avoid it and act if necessary

(2) Reducing energy consumption by optimizing the driving.

Nowadays, global air pollution is serious. (AI) non-manual driving car manufacturers need to concern how to design (AI) machine learning system can reduce degree of air pollution to be the most minimum level to compare to traditional manual driving vehicles.

The reduction of energy consumption if certainly one of the main challenges. Transportation is one of the major factors in fossil energy consumption, and it is also responsible for a large amount of CO2 pollution. It is difficult to ask individuals to voluntarily limit the use of their vehicle of they do not have a strong incentive to do so. Specially in regions where vehicles are needed to drive to go to work every day. It stands to reason that if it is difficult to decrease the amount of vehicles, part of the solution is to make them more energy efficient.

Hence, non-manual driving car manufacturers need to design how to improve engines, which are more optimized and need less fuel to operate, and hybrid and electric cars have been developed and are continuously being improved. But we can go beyond these solutions that do not take into account the environment in which a vehicle is driving. A growing number of scientific contributions presented intelligent systems used in order to improve energy efficiency and reduce fuel consumption, based on the optimization of the way (AI) non-manual driving (AI) vehicles are performing. Such as recharge batteries and electric engine will be predicted the popular fuel in order to limit fuel consumption to future (AI) non-manual driving vehicles. They can reduce air pollution, consume less fuel for (AI) non-manual driving vehicles.

(3) Improving comfort by anticipating (AI) non- manual driving vehicle drivers.

Finally, another application for intelligent vehicle is the improvement of driving comfort. Car industry is very competitive market. Many potentials (AI) intelligent vehicle customers need to enjoy to sit more comfortable intelligent vehicles, who will be attracted by (AI) comfortable systems improving when driving, so part of the research in intelligent systems from cars focuses on how to improve the driving experience, i.e. make it easier and more enjoyable, more comfortable to compare to traditional manual driving vehicles.

As an example, lane keeping assistant systems are technologies that actively keep the vehicle in the lane in highways of the driven drifts out of it. Automatic speed regulation keeps the car at a certain speed without requiring to touch the gas pedal. This can be really interesting for, e.g. (AI) non-manual driving truck drivers that spend a lot of time on highways. But these technologies have a limitation in the case of automatic speed regulation, this technology can not copy of a vehicle ahead drives slower than the desired speed, or if another vehicle cuts into the lane.

This case requires the driver to have a constant focus on the road. In order to achieve more comfort, it is better of the system can adapt to changes in its dynamic environment: let the (AI) intelligent vehicle adapt to the speed of the man-manual vehicle, or autonomously change lane when requires. Again, this requires knowledge about the environment, detection capabilities, reasoning and action planning. Intelligent systems can be used in order to create more attractive and more comfortable and more safe, less energy consumption and less fuel expenditure by intelligent vehicles.

Factors influence public transport service industry reaches life cycle decline stage

In our future road public transport service development. Does underground train improvement bring another new public transport service experience to let passengers to experiece another new road public transport service replace traditional bus, tram, train, taxi , rapid speed train etc. public transport tool service by this kind new " exceed sound speed" underground train public transport tool? Can this kind of " exceed sound speed" underground train public service transport tool replace traditional bus, train, tram, taxi, road piblic transport tools ? Will traditional road public transport tools experience to reach decline life cycle service stage from maturity life cycle service stage in soon future possible, if this kind of " new exceed sound speed innovation underground train is invented ?

What is exceed sound speed underground train ? It can run exceed sound speed to catch above four to eight passengers to sit in the small size circle shape underground train from one distination to another destination in short time. For example, it can run at exceed sound speed at underground from US Washington city to New York city, in the future, it will be possible one kind of small circle size underground train, it may only catch about one to eight passengers every journey, when this kind of new exceed sound speed underground train was really invented. Can it replace traditional slow speed underground train and road public transport tools to be accepted by many passengers?

In this US future new exceed sound speed small size underground train public transport tool case, it only needs spend half hour to transport passengers from US Washington to New York city rapidly. In general, underground train speed needs about three hours from Washington to New York city distance. So, it can shorten time to let passengers to avoid any delay. The question is that : Can it influences future global public transport service life cycle stage to reach decline life service cycle life in short time, if this kind of new exceed sound speed small size underground train public transport tool is invented in success? I shall attempt to answer whether future new sound speed rapid small size underground public tranport service train invention, it will influence other traditional public transport tools to reach the decline life service cycle stage rapidly in short time as below:

In our traditional public transport development history, since 1900, human had been beginning to consider every country ought own themselves public transport fools, e.g. for passengers service. So, passengers can pay cheap ticket to catch either bus, or tram, or train ot ferry, or taxi, or underground train from one destination to another destination in short time conveniently. So, public transport tool needs had been popular increasing, because there were not many people like to buy cars to drive when any kinds of public tranport tools are invented in 1900 beginning. The reason may be that they feel expensive gas expenditure and cars will need to repair or become old etc. different reasons. So, from 1900, public transport tool service tools may be whole public transport service industry's birth life cycle service stage. In this stage, global any passengers had been attempting to choose to catch either bus, trains, trams, taxi, underground trains etc. public transport tools to go to anywhere conveniently. They would compare whether public transport service can provide comfortable feeling and rapid transport service quality to be better than purchase one car to drive.

Hence, in this global public transport service birth life cycle stage, global human had been attempting any kinds of public transport tools catching feeling whether which one kind could bring more comfortable service feeling , e.g. bus service is better or tram service is better or train service is better or underground train service is bettr or ferry service is better. Hence, in global whole public transport industry tools will be compared by all passengers . Passengers will choose the best kind of public transport tool to catch in any time when they feel need. Hence, bus, taxi, train, tram, underground train, ferry transport service performance level must bee very high to avoid their passengers to make decision to choose another kind of public transport service to replace them.

From 1900 to 1950, global public transport service had been experiencing fair or birth stage competition because any one passenger had been attempting to choose which kind of public transport tool to replace purchase car need. After 1950, global public transport service had been experiencing growth life cycle service stage. Because many people began to feel different kinds of public transport tools prices are cheap and reasonable . So global had had many different transport tools to replace purchase cars needs to anyone. Also, bus, taxi, ferry, train, tram , underground train number and transport service frequent time will need to increase in order to satisfy increasing passengers transport service needs in transport service market.

After 1990, global transport service industry had been experiencing mature life cycle service stage, instead of non owning car people must need to catch any kinds of public transport tools to go to aywhere, even owning car people, when they feel that they often drive cars, frequent driving car behavior may bring high gas expenditure in long time. So, when they feel any one kind of transport tool can transport them to go to anywhere conveniently in short time. On the day, they will not drive themselves cars to go to anywhere, they will choose any one kind of public transport tools to go to the destination on that day, because they do not want to spend much gas expenditure or avoid traffic jam or accident occurrence when they need to go to the destination in shor time.

So, in this mature public transport service life cycle stage, global any one includes owning car person and non owning car person, we had been accepted to choose any one kind of public transport tool to replace cars to go to any destinations conveniently. Because bus stations number increased, bus number increases, bus can arrive in short time, taxi, train, tram , ferry , underground train public transport tools services can follow bus service to provide accurate shorten arrival time, comfortable catching environment, reasonable price, none delay arrival time, high passengers transport service quality to let global any one passenger to feel satisfactory. Hence, after 1980, global public transport service had been experiencing mature life cycle service stage.

Global public tranport service needs had been increasing. At the same time, when any one kind of public transport tool is popular to be accepted to choose to catch by any one passenger. In this suitation, if one kind of public transport tool is improved, e.g. shorten transport distance, arrival destination time can be decreased, price is reasonable cheap, such as Japan rapid speed train, China, prior rapid speed train etc. These rapid speed electric trains can transport many passengers from one station to another station in short time. So, in road train service industry, nowadays, it is experiencing mature life cycle service stage. It means that any passengers will be influenced to catch this kind of rapid speed train in prefer to compare tram, traditional old speed train, bus, ferry to catch.

However, in the future, it is possible that one kind of underground train may be invented successfully. It is short circle size underground train, it can catch one to maximum eight passengers only for every journey in underground. Nowadays, US scientists had been attempting to manufacture this kind of " exceed sound speed"' underground train, if it can be invented in success, it may catch maxium eight passengers from Washington to New York city within half hour time . In general, traditional US underground train needs two to three hours to catch passengers from Washington underground train station to New York underground train station. So, if this kind of " exceed sound speed" underground train is invented in success, it will be possible to influence global public transport train, tram, bus, ferry, taxi, public transport tool passengers number may be influenced to reduce, due to its fee is reasonable cheap, more comfortable, rapid destination arrival and on time arrival transport service etc. factors.

The question is that: How this kind of " exceed sound speed underground train tool" bring positive or negative changes to influence global public transport service life cycle stage?

Nowadays, rapid speed train or underground train public service transport tool had changed traditional gas energ train or electric train transport service need to mature life cycle stage. Since electric train or rapid speed train invention. This kind of public transport had provided one kind of more comfortable and rapid transport service choice to any passengers. So, train or underground train transport tool compares to general bus, tram , ferry to experience rapid mature life service cycle stage. Many passengers many feel to catch underground train or train in preference because their ticket prices are reasonable cheap and they are provided rapid short time journey to arrive any destinations any any countries. For London underground is a rapid transit system serving greater histry . These two ran electric trains in circular tunnels having diameters.

In 1933, most of London's underground railways, tramway and bus services are accepted in popular . Hence, UK, LOndon railway public transport tool has developed long time. The average speed on the London underground is 20.5 miles per hour, including station stops. On Metropolitan line, trains can reach over 60 mph. The shortest distance between teo adjacent stations on the network is only 260 metres and the longest is 6.3 kilometres.

Nowadays, the fastest underground train is the Victoria line, it can reach speeds up tp 50 mph because the stations are further apart. The metropolitan line has the fastest train speeds, sometimes reaching over 60 mph. IS light rail faster than buses? IN fact the data is from the National trainsit database website and it shows that it costs almost twice as much, one average to move one light rail vehicle per hour versus onw bus. Hence, light rail must be faster than buses, comparing rail versus bus trainsit transport service life cycle stages, rail versus may reach mature transport service life cycle stage. Otherwise, bus transit transport service life cycle stage will be possible to be influenced to experience decline life service cycle stage from nowadays mature stage. The reason is that future " sound speed underground rail transport will be possibe to invent successfully. Then, this kind improved exceed sound speed underground train transport tool may replace to traditional electric train or underground electric rail, when any countries passengers can accept to choose to catch this kind of developed " exceed sound speed" underground rail tranport tool in habit.

In fact, underground rail versus bus tranit focus primary on vehicle travel speeds and operating, per capita vehicle travel grew rapidly between 1970 and 2000. If one day, US " exceed sound speed" underground short size rail is invented successfully., it will change the whole traditional public tranport service industry mode to persuade passengers to enjoy this kind " exceed sound speed feeling" and choose to catch this kind public transport service in preference, due to they can enjoy rapid short time destination arrival journey, and it can bring benefit to transport providers for lifecycle saving energy and emission carbon pollutants reduces. It may reach the rail public transport tool invention to the topest mature life cycle service stage, if this kind of exceed sond speed underground train can be invented successfully. It means that rail transport service industry only needs to spend less developing time to reach the mature life cycle service stage from birth and growth life cycle service stages .

In global whole public transport service life cycle development stage, underground rail transport tool is the most rapid experiencing the topest mature life cycle service stage of only one kind public transport tool to compare bus, ferry, tram , train . Although, transport infrastructure has long operational life, there are too many urban public transport networks, including light rail (metro and tram), but if the kind of new " exceed sound speed" underground rail can be real invented. Then, in underground rail public transport tool development history, it will help underground electric rail development to let any passengers to feel more comfortable, most rapid, reasonable ticket price and convenient underground journeys in every day. Hence, if it can be invented successfully, it will not only help whole rail transport service to reach mature life service cycle stage or it will be future the best or the most comfortable one kind of using public transport tool choice to global any passengers by 2041. Because when it could real be invented in success, it proved that it may fight physical barriers and fast moving or elevated sound speed levels can cause that any passengers can feel more comfortable and none long time distance to arrive destination anywhere. For example, if this kind of exceed sound speed underground short size rail transport tool can transport US passengers from tunnel to go through ocean to another countries stations. Then, any one does not need to catch airplane transport or ship to go to another country easily. They can catch it to go through ocean underground tunnels to any country from ocean in short time also. So, instead of this kind of sound speed underground rail can replace traditional tram, train, transport service on the road, even it can also replace airplanes and ships, ocean and air transport service by 2041 in the future. So, its transport inventio may change global traditional transport mode, it can provide underground ocean tunnel and underground and tunnel transport channels to arrive any underground road tunnel transport channels to arrive any destinations conveniently. Then, it can bring shop and airplane transport service changes to let wholc passengers to have more one kind of new transport tool choice, such as underground exceed sound speed rail feeling need. So, ship and airplane transport service life cycle may also be influenced to experience decline life cycle service cycle stage after 2041, if this kind of exceed sound speed short circle size underground rail could be invented in success to catch any countries passengers spend short time to catch it to go to another countries' underground rail stations from himself/herself country's underground rail station by ocean tunnel conveniently.

Consequently, future exceed sound speed underground short circle size rail public transport tool invention may influence other kinds of public transport tools to experience and reach decline life cycle service stage early after 2041, if it can real invent successfully by 204. Hence, it explains that why bus, tram, train, ferry, airplane transport tools need to continue to invent or improve rapid flying speed or rapid flight speed and comfortable feeling quality in order to fight this kind of future new exceed sound speed underground rail transport tool to avoid rapid decline life cycle service stage easily after 2041. So, " this kind of exceed sound speed small circle size underground rail" transport tool invention " it will bring global other different kinds of road and sea and air transport tool will face decline life service cycle stage early after 2041 in possible.

Can robot apply to Facility management strategy how assists organizations to
rapid reach to mature life cycle stage

Facility management influences airport and logistic employee performance

● Facility management assists employees reduce
maintenance service expenditure

Facility management provides a variety of non core operations and maintenance services to support any organizations' operation. For logistic organization example, it is possible to provide effective maintenance service to warehouse in order to reduce warehouse facilities to be damaged to bring to spend to buy any new equipment facilities expenditure. So, when the logistic company's warehouse facilities can be maintenance to be the best quality. Then, they can be used these warehouses' machines facilities again. Their performance can assist workers to manufacture any products to keep the most efficiently an raising the best production performance in whole manufacturing process. Then, this logistic company's facility management department can bring to avoid purchase any new machine facilities expenditure spending. One to these warehouses' production machine facilities are kept in the best production performance environment even in long term production need.

I shall indicates airport and warehouse facilities how to influence employees performances as below:

(1) How can comfortable warehouse facilities influence workers' efficiencies in logistic industry ?

The logistic industry's facility management department can create cost savings and efficiency of the warehouse's workplaces. It's machines facilities (production machines) are dealt with the maintenance management of the physical assets maintenance service. FM (facilities management) has been being applied to industrial facilities in logistic and warehouse industry long term as well as maintenance plays a significant role to ensure the full service and the warehousing system, including both building components and equipment in warehouse.

Maintenance service is needed to bring a certain level of availability and reliability of a warehouse facilities system and its components and its ability perform to a standard level of quality. So , it seems that logistic industry's warehouse asset cost reducing. It depends on whether it has one facility management department to provide maintenance service to itself warehouse workplace's production machine facilities and warehouse building itself in order to let workers t feel the manufacturing machines can bring good manufacturing performance to assist them to produce any products in one safe warehouse workplace environment. Hence, the performance measurement of warehouse maintenance issue will be valued to be consider to every warehouse manager and facility manager in logistic industry.

In logistic industry, (FM) works at two level on the one hand, it provides a safe and efficient working environment, which is essential to influence warehouse workers whether how they perform to do their manufacturing tasks or logistic goods delivery tasks in warehouse. When they feel the warehouse is safe environment to work. They will not need to consider anywhere has risk to cause they die by accident in warehouse. Hence, they can concentrate on doing their every tasks . On the other hand, it can involve strategic issues, such as property (warehouse workplace and management, strategy property decision and warehouse facility, e.g. manufacturing machine, facility maintenance and checking planning and maintenance planning development.

However, reducing the operating expense issue will be the main aim when the logistic company feels that it has need to set up one in-house facility management department to carry on any maintenance service for its warehouses' any workplace property and manufacturing machines facilities. So, when the logistic company decides to implement one facility management department, it needs to ensure its facility management department can bring the minimum level of keeping manufacturing performance and efficiency to its warehouses' any manufacturing machines and warehouses' property to avoid to be damaged in short term, such as loss of business due to failure in service, provision of project to customer satisfaction, provision of safe environment, effective utilisation of workplace space, e.g. warehouse effectiveness and communication between the workers and the logistic managers in the warehouse workplace , due to the warehouse's space is not enough maintenance service reliability to the logistic company's warehouse, responsiveness of the warehouse's worker individual negative emotion problem, due to he/she often feels need to work in one unsafe warehouse working environment. Hence, it seems that poor or unsafe warehouse working environment can influence workers feel negative emotion to work to bring low efficiency (inefficiency) or under productive performance in warehouse. It has relationship to influence they to bring psychological negative emotion feeling to work when the organization lacks one effective warehouse management repairing service to be provided to the warehouse's facilities and properties' maintenance needs in order to avoid ineffective measurement and misleading of performance.

Hence, the logistic company's facilities management department often needs to be reviewed whether its maintenance service level is passed to achieve the lowest repair (maintenance) service standard to its warehouse itself property and manufacturing machine or warehouse delivery tool facilities or warehouse lamps' light whether is enough to let workers to see anything clearly to avoid accident occurrence or see anything to work clearly or the warehouse space areas are enough to let they can have enough space to walk or communicate to their team supervisors or deliver any goods more easily in the short distance between the worker's sending goods location and the delivering goods destination in order to avoid because the lacking enough space to cause the accident occurrence , due to the space is not enough to let they deliver their goods to any locations in warehouse.

Hence, it seems logistic company's (FM) department can contribute to the organization's mission, such as avoiding warehouse accident occurrence, inefficiency, not enough and unavailability of the facility for future needs when the warehouse lacks enough space areas to bring poor performance of facility and dangerous warehouse itself property in warehouse, e.g. safe and reliable operations of material handling equipment and maintenance of warehouse facilities, grounds, security system, utilities, plumbing, heating , enough lighting system, air conditioning, warming heater, fire protection, security system alarm etc. facilities in warehouse.

Hence, it seems that if the logistic company expected to reduce to spend lot of excessive manufacturing machine purchase expenditure, lose of workers' life or bring workplace accidents , due to poor warehouse workplace environment, even bringing lawsuit compensation claim loss , due to the worker individual accident or death is caused from the poor warehouse facilities, or bring negative emotion to let the workers feel they are working in unsafe warehouse workplace environment. Then, it ought choose to set up on facility management department in order to provide enough maintenance service to its warehouse to avoid these non essential expenditure causing , due to these poor warehouse facilities factors.

Hence any logistic company ought choose to set up one itself in -house facility management department, it be better than outsourcing its all facilities service to one facility management (maintenance service provider) to help it to deal any kinds of maintenance service in warehouse. Because it is long term maintenance need to its warehouse's any machines and warehouse itself properties. If it chose to find one outsourcing facilitiy management maintenance service provider to replace its in-house facility management department to deal all related facilities maintenance tasks in warehouse. Then, it is possible that it needs to pay long time facilities maintenance service fee to its outsourcing facility management maintenance service provider more than itself facility management maintenance service provision department.

(2) Can facility management influence tourism industry's human resource management influence to improve productivity in airline, travel agent, hotel tourism sectors?

In tourism industry, measuring productivity froma HRM prespective is extremely difficult and has proven to be a limitation within the tourism sector. Due to the customers are not tangible. For example, how can the travel agent measure its travel consultant individual service performance to evaluate whether the travelling customer feels or does not feel satisfactory loyalty from his/her service? How can the airline measure its pilot , airline front-line travelling passenger service attendant indiviual service performance to evaluate whether his/her travelling passenger feels or does not feel satisfactory to whose service performance? Whether airport facility management can influence airline counter service staffs performance ?

However, the complaint number whether it is more or less to the airline or travel agent's service behavior , it does not represent whose service attitude or behavior or performance is poor absolutely because there are many travelling consumers whose complaints are unreasonable , although they feel satisfactory to the airline attendent or airline front -line service staffs individual service performance, but if they feel unhappy to be caused by the airline or travel agent service staff. They will still compain their performance. For this suitation example , it is possible that the travelling passenger is delayed to catch the airplance to fly, due to the country's sudden worse weather influnce, he/she will complain the airline fron-line counter travelling customer service staffs, it concerns when the air plane will arrive the airport, if the airline counter service staff's feedback is that the airplane needs long time arrival. Then, the travelling passengers will complain to the airline counter service staffs in angry. But in fact, the air plane delays to arrive the airport, the airline counter service staffs ought not need responsibilitie to explain the reason why they can not assist the delayed air plane to arrive the country in easier. Furthermore, thy will be complained unreasonably. Hence, it is difficult to measure tourism sector's service staffs 'performance, also the complaint exact number is not one judgement factor to measure their service performance absolutely.

I assume any tourism industry's front -line service airline staffs, they must attempt to serve their travelling passenger in positive service attitude and behavior. So, any tourism industy, how to improve their front -line service staff performance in order to let they to know how to deal unreasonable complaints in sudden unpredictive suitation. Their training materials or contents my include: Teaching them how to provide positive feedback to treat any travelling passenger individual difficult problems or unreasonable complaints in order to reduce their psychological pressure to unknown how to treat these passenger individual related problems when they are facing in airports or travelling agent workplaces. The travelling agent or airline travelling service organizations can attempt to collect measures of employee performance from customers , for example, comment cards in hotel rooms, airplane, travel agent's workplace, mystery shoppers etc. more focus shouls be pleased on this form of evaluation. In order to evaluate the actually place value on the customer ratings to every employee. The all every day, the form of evaluation concerning the actually value on the customer ratings , will be gathered to strategic , it has how many customers feel good or bad ratings to every employee individual performance when every one's tasks are finishing. Due to one month, it can make statistic report to calculate how much performance marks to give to every employee in order to evaluate whether every one's performance is satisfactory to be accempted to the lowest level. If the employee's marks rating is low, his/her department manager can arrange a time and day to meet him/her to discuss whether which aspects of problems who feels in order to give recommendation how to improve his/her service attitude to let customer to give higher marks rating to him/her next time.

Hence tourism industry's service sector organizations need to have one training department to arrange courses how to improve employee service performance in order to let customer to give higher marks rating to very one as well as finding methods how to excite every front line service employee individual loyalty , they can increase their confidence to know how to deal sudden unreasonable complaints in effective and efficient positive attitude. In conclusion, how to improve employee service performance issue will be any tourism service organization's HRM concerning problem. Airports need to arrange how to implement efficient and comfortable and available convenient airport facilities to let any airline service counter staffs feel enjoyable to serve their passengers. They need to know how to find the most effective methods to solve how improvement of front line employee individual performance problem in order to raise the airline or travel agent's quality of service to let itself further customers to feel its service performance is better than others. So, facility management has indirect relationship to influence airport airline service staffs performances.

In conclusion, to decide whether the company ought need or not need facilities maintenance service or either set up in-house facility management department or outsource one facility management maintenance service provider. It depends on whether its organization has how many facilities are used in its workplace, how many staffs are working the workplace, how much size of its workplace, its workplace is office or warehouse or factory, how long time of its facilities' useful time etc. factors , then it can decide whether it needs or does not need one facility maintenance service department or outsourcing facility maintenance service provider to help it to deal any facilities management problem in its organization.

● Facility management role in organization

When one company feels that it has need facility management service. It can choose to set up either in-house facility management department or seek one outsourcing facility management service provider to help it to arrange any facility management service need. However, this facility management role is only one for the organization. It concerns this question: What facility management maintenance function can bring the benefits to the organization?

It can define that all services required for the management of building and real estate to maintain and increase their value, the means of providing maintenance support, project management and user management during the building life cycle, the integration of multi-disciplinary activities within the built environment and the management of their impact upon people and the workplace. In traditional, (FM) services may include building fabric maintenance, decoration and refurbishment, plant, plumbing and drainage maintenance, air conditioning maintenance, lift and escalator maintenance , fire safety alarm and fire fighting system maintenance, minor project management. All these are hard services. Otherwise, cleaning , security, handyman services, waste disposal, recycling, pes control, grounds maintenance, internal plants. All these are soft services. Additional services, might also include: pace planning, things moving management, business risk assessment, business continuity planning, benchmarking, space management, facilities contract outsourcing service arrangement, information systems, telephony, travel booking facility utility management, meeting room arrangement services, catering services, vehicle fleet management, printing service, postal services, archiving , concierge services, reception services, health and safety advice, environmental management.

All of these services will be every organization's in-house facility soft or hard services needs. So, it explains why some large organizations feel need one effective facility management department to help them to arrange how to implement facility services efficiently in order to achieve cost reducing, raising efficiency and performance improvement aims because one effective facility management control system can influence employee individual productive effort to be raised or reduced indirectly.

However, (FM) can be selected either setting up one in-house (FM) department or outsourcing its services to one facility management service provider to help the organization to solve any kinds of facilities maintain service problems. One on-house (FM) department is a team, it needs employees to deliver all (FM) services. Some specialist services are needed to be outsourced, when the service is on expertise in the company. The no expertise services will be outsourced to simple service contracts, e.g. lift and escalator (FM) department will have direct labour, but it can outsource some specialist to help it to do some complex facilities management service. So, the team leader can of can manage whose team staffs, such as maintenance technicians run low risk operations . Otherwise, the outsourcing facility management service provider needs to help it to operate high risk operations or maintenance vital plant facility management service. Anyway, it can set up in-house (FM) department to arrange specialist direct labour and outsourced (FM) services to more than one facility management service providers to do different kinds of (FM) services. One of these outsourcing (FM) service provider, who can arrange sub-contractors to assist it to finish any (FM) services of it's outsourcing (FM) services are more complex to compare the other sub-contractors (third parties).

● What is a facility manager's role to provide quality service to satisfy its user needs?

We need to know how quality can be defined in facility management and why it should be defined by the customer? How facility managers can find out customer (user) needs? What are the difficulties in finding out users' needs and in delivering quality services? Whether improving quality always means requiring higher cost?

In general, facility manager's major responsibilities may include these major functional areas: longer range and annual facility planning, facility financial forecasting, real estate acquisition and/or disposal, work specification, installation and space management, architectural and engineering planning and design, new construction and/or renovation, maintenance and operations management, maintenance and operation management, telecommunications integration, security and general administrative services. When the facility manager had implemented any one of these FM services for those user. How does he/she provide excellent (FM) service quality ot let whose users to feel satisfactory?

In fact, quality issues can not be considered without customer-oriented perspective service quality involves a comparison of expectation with performance. (FM) service quality is a measure of how well to service level delivered matches customer expectation. So, these issues are (FM) service user's general measurement level requirement. The (FM) manager needs to achieve these the minimum performance measurement level to satisfy whose (FM) user's needs.

However, (FM) service quality has three characteristics: Intangibility, heterogeneity, inseparability. But in fact, (FM) service delivered may be through tangible physical aspects, e.g. factory plant workplace building, machine equipment maintenance, intangible (FM) services, e.g. managing space moving in plant to let staffs to work, managing outsourcing cleaners to clean factory equipment. However, all (FM) service performance often varies, due to the behavior of service personnel. Hence, a well developed job specification and training can help to improve the consistence of services of (FM). Any (FM) production and consumption of many services may are inseparable and they are usually interactions between the (FM) client and the contact person from the service provider.

Hence, it seems that service quality is considered as hard to evaluate. In (FM) service quality, it includes physical quality and interactive non-physical service quality. Physical quality is tangibles: The appearance of the physical facilities, equipment, personnel and communication materials. Non-physical services quality means reliability: The ability to perform the promised service dependably and accurately; responsiveness means the willingness to help customers and provide prompopt service to let user to feel; assurance mans the competence of the system in its credibility in providing a courteous and secure service and empathy means the approachability, ease of access and effort taken to understand customers' needs.

Hence, a good performance of (FM) manager , he/she ought satisfy the user's tangible and non-tangible both service quality needs. I recommend that he/she can attempt to predict what are the (FM) customer expects in each (FM) service needs. Then, it can make decision what aspect(s) will be the (FM) users major (FM) service need and what aspect(S) won't be the (FM) users major (FM) service need. Then, he/she can make more accurate decision to arrange time, human resource , cost spending amount arrangement whether when it ought concentrate on finishing the (FM) major service tasks as well as whether how he/she ought finish the major (FM) service tasks to be more easily, e.g. how to arrange staffs number to finish, how many the minimum staffs number is needed to be arrange the major (FM) service tasks, time arrangement is important factor, because it can influence whether he/she ought finish the major (FM) service tasks today or tomorrow or later in order to have enough time to finish other non-major (FM) service tasks. Instead of time management, staff number arrangement is also important factor , if he/she arranged the excessive staffs number to do the (FM) major services tasks, then it is possible that it will have shortage of staffs number to finish the non-major (FM) service tasks on the day. So, avoiding either major or non-major (FM) services can not finish on the day. The (FM) manager needs to predict when the major (FM) services and the non-major (FM) services which are necessary to be finished in order to have enough time and staffs to assist him/her to finish every day major and non-major (FM) service effectively. Then, the achievement of his/her (FM) major and non-major tangible and non-tangible services , it will have more chance to be performed efficiently by his/her managed staffs.

In conclusion, in any organizations , (FM) manager needs have good predictable effort to evaluate whether when his/her managed team need to finish the major and/or non-major (FM) tasks as well as whether how he/she ought arrange the accurate time and staff number to finish any major and/ or non-major (FM) service tasks on the day. Then, his/her leading of (FM) service team can be managed to work more efficiently in order to satisfy her/his (FM) service user's needs.

Facility management how influences
public service transport service performance

● How (FM) space moving management brings employees efficiencies
There are interesting questions: How (FM) can bring value-add to avoid loss or earn more profit to the organization? Can it influence employees to raise performance and improve efficiency ? Some organizations' (FM) service need which is necessary in order to let employees can raise productivity.

It is based on these assumptions: I assume the organizations have completely either outsourced or in-house their (FM) facility management departments will gain more effect on added value than they have no (FM) function as well as organizations have a strong coordination with the (FM) department will gain more added value than organizations with a weak coordination. Organizations in the profit aim can gain more added value than organizations in the not for profit aim sectors.

In fact, any organization is difficult to confirm it has relationship between improving performance, raising efficiency and owning (FM) function in its organization. (FM) could have to do with the attraction of easy but incomplete indicators of efficiency rather than the necessarily and less direct measures if the effectiveness and the relevance of space moving useful management, e.g. whether building has the enough space to let employees to move to work easy in order to raise efficiency, whether the building has excessive furniture and equipment number and they are putted on wrong places to be caused employees move difficulty in the building in order to influence productive performance.

However, how to arrange space moving management to equipment, e.g. copying machines, faxes, productive machines, they are putted on the locations where have enough space to let employees to move to another locations. For example, the building floor has more than 50 employees, but its space is not enough to let these 50 employees to move to any locations to let them to feel easily often. Then, it is possible to cause they feel nervous pressure and they can feel difficult to work , when they are working in a small office space or factory space or warehouse space. Then, the consequence will be under-predictive efficiency or poor performance to any one of these 50 employees in this office or factory or warehouse.

" Facility management is responsible for coordinating all efforts related to planning, designing, and managing buildings and their systems, equipment, and furniture to enhance. The organizations abilty to compete successfully in a rapidly changing world." (F.Becker)

The author explains equipment, workplace internal space designing, furniture space putting location arrangement will have possible to influence employee individual productive performance or efficiency to be raised or reduced in the workplace. Hence, it seems that, in the value chain (FM) belongs to the activity part of the firm. To make the facilities cooperation with each office or factory or warehouse using space moving facility management. Facility space moving management must be linked strategically, tactically and operationally to other support activity to add value to the organization's office or factory or warehouse space moving management arrangement more effectively.

Thus, how to arrangement space moving management issue it will have possible to influence the organization's employee individual productive performance and efficiency in whose workplace. It seems that (FM) space moving management arrangement have indirect relationship to influence the organization's employee individual performance and efficiency , due to they need often to work in the workplace, if they feel moving difficulty , or excessive equipment , furniture number is putting into the small office, factory or warehouse locations, or they feel the office or factory or warehouse has excessive (a lot of) staffs number to work in the small space of office or factory or warehouse. Then, they can not concentrate nervous on finishing every tasks in possible. In long term, their efficiencies will be poor or inefficiencies or their performance won't be improved or causing poor performance in possible.

Instead of the not enough space moving and excessive staffs number factor, it will bring another question: Can enough information systems equipment cause a more efficient and improved performance to the organization staffs in the workplace?

I assume that the office has 100 employees and it has only ten copying machines. So it means that ten employees use one copying machine. Hence, it brings this question: Is it enough to provide only ten copying machines to average ten employees to use? It depends on other factors, e.g. whether any one of these 100 employees needs to print how many documents per day , whether the five copying machines' locations are far away to separate different locations or they are stored in one printing room in the office, whether the day has how many staffs are absent, whether the day has how many printing machine(s) is/ are broken to need to be repaired. Hence, these unpredictable external environment factors will influence whether the five copying machines number is enough to let these 100 employees to use in the office every day. Hence, facility manager ought need to spend to observe average their copying behaviors every day in order to make data record. Many employees need to use copy machines to print documents, average how many document's page number, they need to print, how much average time spending to print their documents, average how many staff absent number on the day. Even, if the all five copying machines are stored in the printing room, calculating the staffs number whether how many staffs need more than five minutes to walk to the printing room to print their documents many staffs need to spend five minute to walk to the printing room, and they have other urgent tasks to wait to finish. It is possible to influence their efficiency, due to they often need to spend more than five minutes to walk to the printing room to print documents. If there are many staffs need to often to print documents, but their printing task will have many time, e.g. 20 separate printing tasks. Then, they need to spend at least (20x5) 100 minutes to spend time to walk to the printing room to print their documents. It must influence that they should not finish the other urgent tasks on the day. If there are many staffs to spend much time to walk to the printing room in the least 20 separate printing time or more on that day. All the facility manager needs to evaluate whether all the five copy machines are stored in the printing room whether it is the best location decision or they ought need be separated to put on different office locations in their workplaces, even he/she ought need to evaluate whether it is enough copying machines number, when the office has only 5 copying machines. He/she ought need to buy more copying machines number to satisfy any one of these 100 employee individual copying task need.

In conclusion, effective office or factory or warehouse space moving facility management will be one part task of (FM) function. If the office or factory or warehouse can have accurate equipment, machine , furniture number to avoid excessive or shortage number problem to cause employees often feel moving difficult problem in their workplace when they need to move to another location to work in office or warehouse or factory as well as whether the staff needs often spend time to wait the another employee to use the copying machine to print whose document or fax machine to deliver whose document. Then, it is not that fax or printing machines number is not enough to provide the employees to use in the office or warehouse or factory workplace.

Hence, (FM) includes space moving facility management to equipment , machines, furniture number as well as choosing anywhere is(are) the suitable location (s) arrangement to putting or storing these facilities in workplace as well as decision of the staff number and the workplace area size whether it has excessive staffs number to cause these staffs need to work in the small area size of office or warehouse or factory workplace. So, the organization ought need to decide whether it needs to reduce the office's staffs number to let them to work in another more suitable locations in another workplace. Hence, all these facilities space moving management and staffs and workplace size issues will be (FM) manager's consideration issues, because these external environment factors will influence employee individual efficiency and performance to be poor to cause low valued to its organization in long term in possible .

● Predictive the choosing right
data asset and (FM) analytics
solutions to boost public
transportation service quality

Can gather the choosing right data public transportation service station facilities asset and analytics, it can give recommendation to help any organization to boost service quality? (FM) analytics data can be applied to public transportation service industry to be supported how and why the train, train, ferry , ship, air plane, underground train public transportation tools' time arrival and leaving information notice board and automated ticket paying machines facilities are putting on or stored any where locations in order to boost passengers to feel their facilities locations are convenient to let them to buy tickets and see the arrival and leaving time for the next public transportation tool from the information notice electronic board machine. So, it seems that these public transportation tools' station facilities locations can influence passengers to feel the public transportation service company how to consider to its passenger's buying ticket needs and next public transportation tool's arrival and leaving time information needs in order to boost its passengers use service quality and let them to feel better service reliable performance in any train, tram, ferry , ship, underground tram, airplane stations.

As these public transportation service organizations need to learn data analytics represent an opportunity for its ticket paying machine equipment facilities as well as the next transportation tool arrival and leaving time information notice board electronic equipment facilities anywhere the locations are the most suitable to put on or store these equipment to let passengers to walk to the ticket paying machines to buy the ticket to catch the train, tram, underground train, ferry, airplane, taxi, ship more easily. So, they do not need to spend more time to find these facilities locations and spend more time to queue to wait to buy ticket to catch the public transportation tool in stations conveniently. Instead of where is the seeking ticket paying machine location, where is the next public transportation tool arrival and leaving information notice time , these both issues will be any public transportation tool's passenger's main needs.

Hence, how to spend time to seek where the next public transportation tool's arrival and leaving time information electronic notice machine location and where the ticket paying machine location , these both factors will influence any passengers' positive or negative emotion causing. For example, if the passenger feels difficult to find the ticket paying machine in the large area size train station or /and he/she feels difficult to find the train time arrival and leaving information to let him/her to know when the next train will arrive the station. Due to he/she feels difficult to find the train ticket paying machine, he/she needs to spend much time to find any one ticket paying machine in the train station. Then, it will influence him/her to choose another public transportation tool to replace the train public transportation tool, e.g. he/she can choose to catch tram, underground train, taxi, bus, ferry, taxi, ship to replace train. So, it seems ticket paying machine and time arrival and leaving information notice electronic equipment 's location putting or stored choice will be one factor to influence the passenger to choose another kind of public transportation tool to replace train at the moment. When, he/she feels that he/she arrives the destination in the most short time. Then, the public transportation service organization (FM) manager has responsibility to evaluate whether there are enough ticket paying machines number to let passengers do not need to spend more time to queue to buy tickets to catch the public transportation tool in short time as well as there are enough time arrival and leaving for next transportation tool to let passengers to know. It will be their concerning issues when they arrive the public transportation service tool's station.

Hence, predictive passenger individual walking behavior can help the public transportation service organization to choose whether where are the most convenient and attractive locations to let the ticket paying machines and the arrival and leaving time information electronic board machines to be putted on or stored in the suitable station positions in order to let many passengers can find these essential facilities in stations very easily. So, gathering data concerns passenger walking behavior in the public transportation service any stations, which can help the facility manager to make more accurate evaluation to attempt to predict whether where the locations are common places to let passengers to choose to walk daily or where the locations are not common places to let passenger to choose not to walk daily in general. Then, he/she can apply these data of different locations in the stations to evaluate whether anywhere they will have many passengers to choose to walk or whether anywhere they won't have many passengers to choose to walk in order to make more accurate decision whether anywhere are the most suitable locations to let the ticket paying machines and the time arrival and leaving information electronic board equipment to be putter on or stored in order to let them to feel it is so easier to let them to find.

Anyway, calculating each station's passenger number per day issue is important to predict whether where , there are many passengers choose to walk or where, there are not many passengers choose to walk in these different public transportation service stations in order to evaluate whether where the stations' different ought put on paying ticket machines or time arrival and leaving information electronic boards in order to let they feel very easy to buy tickets and seeing the next arrival and leaving time information for the kind of public transportation service tool conveniently in the different stations. Moreover, if the station has no enough ticket paying machines number to be supplied to let passengers need to spend more than ten minute time to wait to buy ticket to catch the kind of public transportation service tool in every queue every day. Then it will cause them to choose another kind of public transportation tool to catch go to working place or entertainment place to replace it to on that day. Then, it will cause these passengers who often do not like to queue in the kind of public transportation service tool's any stations, who will not choose to go to anywhere of this kind of public transportation service tool's any stations again. Hence, in long term this kind of public transportation service tool will lose many passengers. Thus, calculating each station's busy time of passengers number , which can predict when it is the busy time and it can make more accurate decision whether the station has need to increase enough ticket paying machines number in order to bring enough supply number to satisfy passengers' ticket purchase need in the busy time.

In conclusion, gathering above all stations' public transportation service equipment facilities number, storing positions data and every station's passenger walking behavior data, they are necessary to any public transportation tool service industry, because these equipment number and storing locations will influence them to make decisions to choose another kind of public transportation tool to replace it's transportation service if they often feel difficult to find these facilities in its different stations. Thus, it is part of task to facility manager's responsibility if the public transportation service organization expects it won't lose many passengers , due to these external environment factor influence and it also implies cheap ticket price does not guarantee the passengers will choose to catch this kind of public transportation service tool to go to anywhere.

● The relationship between facility
management and productive
efficiency

It is one interesting question: Can facility management function bring benefits to raise productive efficiency to organizations? I shall indicate some cases to attempt to explain this possible occurrence chance as below:

● Facility management benefit to office workplace

In private organizations, when the firm has facility management department, whether it can bring efficient administration to influence clerks to work efficiently in office, e.g. reducing administrative time or shorten time to work in administrative processes, in order to achieve minimizing clerk number labor cost. How to design office facilities to let office staffs to feel comfortable to work and reducing their pressure to work. It seems that office working environment will influence office staff individual performance. If the office working environment could improve efficiency and creativity of services to satisfy office workers' comfortable working environment needs. It will reduce every administration manager's working pressure when he/she needs often to find methods to attempt to encourage whose administrative clerks to avoid to waste working time to do some non-major administration tasks.

Hence, how to design or allocate or arrange office any facilities' stored locations or whether how many equipment number is the enough to store in the locations, which will influence office employees' working attitude in order to raise or reduce their administration tasks efficiency indirectly, e.g. the office is clean or dirty, whether office reception has enough information telephone switchboard operation facilities, whether every clerk's table has enough computers number to supply to every to use, whether internet speed is fast or slow in order to let any employees can send and receive email to communicate or download any document from internet in short time, whether data processing and computer system maintenance service supply is enough to be repaired to employees' computers immediately when their computers are broken to wait repair, whether website editing facilities operation whether is enough to link to office every staffs in order to let any office staffs can apply internet to do their tasks conveniently in short time. Hence, all of these general office equipment facilities whether they are enough supplied and their stored positions anywhere are the suitable to assist any clerks to work conveniently, they will influence every office employee's administrative and productive efficiency indirectly as well as all faxes, copying machines, computers, whether internet linking maintenance service time is short or long to prepare to any office employees to use conveniently any time, these different issues will also influence every employee individual efficiency in office. Hence, it concludes that office working environment, facilities supply number, facilities maintenance service and facilities location storing both factors will influence employee individual administrative productive efficiency in office.

● facility management benefits to service working environment

Can effective facility management improve service working environment to raise employee individual work performance? It is a concern about the quality of service to its customer question. The term" standards and goals" are often used to measure staff individual service performance whether he/she can serve to customers to let them to feel this staff's service performance or attitude is good or bad.

Is the service workplace working environment facilities enough, it will influence customer service staff individual performance.

For shopping center service industry case example, for this situation, e.g. shopping center's facilities are enough or are placed to the suitable locations in order to let the shopping center's customers to feel comfortable to shopping when they enter this shopping center as well as whether the shopping center's facilities can influence the customer service staffs to serve whose shopping customers easily or difficult, due to whether the shopping center's facilities whether are adequate supplied or their locations are the best suitable positions to influence their service performance to let them to feel easier or comfortable to serve their customers in any large size shopping centers. For example, whether the lamps' lighting energy is enough to let the shoppers to feel safe to walk to visit any shops when there are many shoppers were walking to cause crowd and they feel difficult to walk to avoid any body contact to any one in busy time when the shopping center has no enough lights to let them to see anywhere in the shopping center's dark environment. Then it will influence customer service staffs to feel difficult to find any shopping center customers, e.g. when two shopping center customers are fighting in one location where is far away to the shopping customer service staffs and securities in the shopping center, because the shopping center is large and it has no enough light to let the customer service staffs and securities to find their frighting location to deal their fighting behavior and other shopping center's shoppers will feel very dangerous to walk their fighting location to avoid to close them. Then, it will has possible to cause death or hurt to any one of these two fighting shoppers ,even other shoppers' life. Because the shopping center's securities and customer service staffs who need to spend much time to find their fighting location, it will delay they can bring the policemen to their fighting location when they arrive this shopping center's destination in short time in order to solve their fighting behavior to influence all shoppers' life in this shopping center. Hence, the shopping center whether it has enough lamps number and the lamps' light whether is enough, these lighting facilities will influence any shopping center customer service staffs and securities who can spend less time to arrive any locations to deal any urgent matters.

For another situation in shopping center, if the shopping center has no enough paying telephone service facilities to supply shoppers to phone to anyone when they feel need to phone to any in the shopping center. Then, it will lead to some shoppers decide to find where the shopping center's reception's telephone to supply to them to phone call to anyone. If they are ten shoppers are waiting to use the shopping center's reception telephone to phone call to their friend or family within one minute. Thus, it will influence the reception customer service staffs feel difficult to arrange how to distribute the only one telephone to these ten shoppers to use to phone call their friend or family when they are queuing within their one minute waiting time in the shopping center's reception. If these ten shoppers can not use the reception telephone to phone call anyone. hen, they will feel dissatisfactory and complain to the reception service staffs politely. So, lacking enough facilities in the shopping center's any where, it will possible to influence their shopping centers' shoppers to feel all shopping center's service staff individual performance to be poor. It means that if the shopping center expects to improve customer satisfaction to its customer service staff's behavioral performance, it meets have enough facilities to be supplied in the shopping center to let its shoppers to feel it is one comfortable and safe shopping center. In conclusion, shopping center's facilities will have possible to influence shoppers' feeling to evaluate its customer service staffs to evaluate whether their service attitudes are good or poor indirectly.

● Can facility management improve productivity

The productivity means resources (input) is therefore the amount of products or services (output), which is produced by them. Hence, higher (improved) productivity means that more is produced with the same expectation of resource, i.e. at the same cost is terms of land materials, machine, time or labor. Alternatively, it means same amount is produced at less labor cost in term of land, material, machine, time for labor that is utilized. So, it brings this question: How can facility management improve productivity? I shall explain as these several aspects, it is possible to be improved productivity from (FM) successfully.

Improved productivity of farm land: If the farming land has better facility management to bring advantages by using better seed, better facilities of cultivation and most fertilizer. It is in the agricultural sense is increased (improved). So, facility management can bring benefits to any land resource to raise productivity in possible. It implies that the productivity of land used for better facility management of industrial purposes is said to have been increased if the output of products or service within that area of industrial land is increased output aim.

Improved productivity of material: If the factory has improved better equipment by facility management method to assist skillful workers to raise the manufacture cloth number, then the productivity of the cloth number is improved by (FM) method.

Improved productivity of labour: When the factory has good manufacturing equipment facilities to be supplied to improve methods of work to product more producing number per hour, then (FM) improved productivity of worker. Hence, in any workplaces, when organization has good facilities, it will influence employees to raise productivities in possible, because they need often to improved equipment facilities manufacture products to achieve higher production number aim.

● Can facility management raise bank employee productivity

Bank workplace environment is busy, the bank counter service staffs need to contact many bank clients to help them to serve or withdraw money from bank's counters. Whether does the quality of environment in bank workplace will influence the determination level of employee's motivation, subsequent performance productivity in bank working environment. For example, if the bank's staffs need work under inconvenient conditions , it will bring low performance and face occupational health diseases causing high absenteeism and turnover.

In general, bank size is usually small, it will have many bank clients enter bank to contact counter staffs to need them to help them to save or withdraw money. So, it will bring air pollution the crowd queue in every bank counter challenge when the bank has many people are queue waiting in counters to queue. So, bank working condition problem relates to environmental and physical factors which will influence every bank counter staff individual working performance to serve bank clients satisfactory. However, bank staffs need to deal many documents concern every client personal data every day. So, they need to spend much time to use computer and painting machines. This is particularly true for these employees who spend most of the day operating a computer terminal in bank workplace. As more and more computers are being installed in workplaces, an increasing number of business has been adopting designs for bank offices installment. So, bank needs have effective facilities management design because of demand of bank staffs for more human comfort.

An good equipment facility management for bank staffs to use conveniently, it is assumed that better workplace environment can motives bank employees and produces better productivity. Hence, bank office environment can be described in terms of physical and behavioral components to influence bank staffs to work inefficiently. To achieve high level of bank employee productivity, bank organizations must ensure that the physical environment in conductive to bank different department organizational needs, facilitating interaction and privacy, formality and informality, functional and disciplinarily, e.g. house loan or private loan departments, counter service department, visa card application department.

Thus, in a high safe privacy facility management working environment will let different department bank staffs feel safe to worry about privacy loss in possible. So, the improving bank facility to bring safe and high privacy to avoid bank client individual loss in working environment issue, the facility management can be results to bring these benefits, such as in a reduction in a number of complaints and absenteeism and an increase in productivity.

● Can (FM) create value to organization?

(FM) can reduce managing facilities as a strategic resource to add value to the organization and its overall performance, e.g. saving the energy in building and take care of shuttle buses and parking facilities space management for , on economic efficiency and effectiveness, or good price and value for the organization.

If the organization expects to apply (FM) process to save energy, it depends on possible input factors, i.e. interventions in the accommodation facilities services. So, it seems that the organization expects to save its energy consumption in its building. It needs have good space management facilities between parking its shuttle buses in its property's car park.

Why does space facility management is important to influence efficiency and productivity. For one school's building example, when the school decides none of the two gymnasiums student sport entertainment centers to be built in order to reduce financial cost and higher benefits. Remarkably, the use of space with the school overall strategic goals , such as creating spaces that better can support the teaching, motivate students and teachers, attract more students and increase the utilisation of existing space to accommodate an increasing number of students.

If it hopes to make high quality teaching facilities on student's choice where to study. The school will need to choose to build either one comfortable and new design facility teaching accommodation or build two gymnasium sport entertainment centers in its limited land space either for students' learning or sport aim. Due to it feels new teaching accommodation can make more attractive to increase students numbers to choose it to study more than building two new gym sport centers to let them do sport in school.

Hence, space choice (FC) management strategy will be one important considerable issue, when the organization has limited land space resources to make choose to build any constructions in order to increase many clients number. Such as the school organization has limited storage land resource to let it to build either two gymnasium sport entertainment centers or one new teaching accommodation in order to attract many students to choose it to learn. Hence, it needs to gather data to make more accurate evaluation to decide how to apply its space facility to choose to build these both kinds of buildings in order to achieve the attractive student learning choice aim, so whether the two sport entertainment activity centers or one new teaching accommodation choice, it needs to gather information to decide whether the school ought to choose to build which kind of building in order to achieve the increase of student number aim, so space facility management will be this school's land shortage problem.

● The relationship between facility
management and consumer
behavior

How and why shop facility management can influence consumer individual shopping behavior? If it is possible, what shop facility management factors can influence their consumption decision when they enter the shop to plan to buy anything. I shall indicate some shop case studied to explain whether how and why every shop's facility management can influence consumer individual consumption desire when any one consumer enters any shops.

● Shop's low ceiling height location (FM) influence consumer behavior
Can the shop's ceiling height influence shoppers' shopping behavior? Can the shop's variation in ceiling height can influence how consumers process information to decide to make purchase decision in the shops, e.g. for this situation, when the consumer enters the shop, he/she feels the ceiling height is low and it has a lamp will contact his/her head in possible. So, he/she chooses to move far away from the low ceiling location in the shop. It is possible that shop's ceiling low height and the lamp locates at the ceiling low height position will influence many customers' choices to leave the low ceiling height and lamp location, then the shop's low ceiling height will have possible to influenced many customers to choose to find the another shop to buy the similar kind of products , due to the lamp locates in the low ceiling height, so this lamp and low ceiling height will be possible factor to influence any shoppers who won't choose to walk to this dangerous location in the shop. If the shop's all spaces are ceiling height and it has many lamps are located at the low ceiling height spaces. Then, it will be serious to cause many shoppers do not want to spend too much time to choose any products

in the shop because they feel dangerous to walk to the any low ceiling height lamps' locations in the shop.

Hence, hoe to design the different concept may be activated by the showroom ceiling if it were relatively high, as it tends to be in mall stores, versus low, as it is in most strip mall shops and outlet centers. Relatively high ceilings may bring safe shopping emotion to let any consumers to feel thoughts related to freedom, whereas lower ceilings may let consumers to feel dangerous to walk the locations in any shops. Hence it seems any shops ought not neglect whether their ceiling height is tall and the lamps ought avoid to locate in any low ceiling height locations in order to influence consumers number to be decreased.

● Can house facility management influence consumer individual purchase intention?

When one new property is built, whether the property consumers will consider how the new property is facility to influence their purchase intention to the property will the new property's (FM) influence buyers in real estate markets' preferences choice and living interest. Any new property's internal characteristics of the house unit itself , such as rooms available, when example, of external are location, accessibility to utilities services and facilities will have possible to influence the property buyer's final property purchase decision, so it seems that even the property price is cheap, it is not represent the property buyer will choose to buy the property, if he/she feels the property's facility management is poorer to compare other similar kinds of properties.

So, it can help real estate analysts better explain and predict the behavior of decision makers in real estate markets. Property consumers will search for property information, concerns the property's quality, price distinctiveness, ability, facility management, service of the property's external environment to decide whether the property is high value to choose to buy to compare other kinds of properties.

However, the external environmental forces, such as limited resources, e.g. time or financial will influence whose property consumption choice and living the property's satisfaction feeling (represent) a feedback from post-property purchase reflection used to inform subsequent decisions. The process of the property buyer's leaving experience will serve to influence the extent to which the property consumer how to consider future next time property purchases decision and new information methods. Hence, when one property consumer chooses to buy a house, it refers house features are house internal attributes , such as quality of building, the design as well as internal and external design, which are important factors for a property consumer when he/she needs to select and purchases one house.

The other (FM) factors which can influence the property consumers' needs, include living space as features, such as the size of kitchen, bathroom, bedroom, living bath and other rooms available in the house. The environment of housing area is also important factor, e.g. the condition of the hood, attractiveness of the area, quality of houses, type of houses, type of houses, density of housing, wooded area or free coverage, slope of the attractive views, open space, non-residential uses in the areas vacant sites, traffic noise, level of owner-occupation in , level of education in level of income in, security from crime, quality of schools, religious of , transportation , shopping center, sport entertainment can be supplied to close to the house area. All these human related issue of the property's location will also influence the property buyer's living location selection. Hence, above (FM) influence property consumer purchase behavior, it is based on the relationship behavior. The consumer's house purchase intention and house features, living space, environment and distance to recreation center, supermarket, library etc. public facilities variable (FM) factors.

In conclusion, the house internal space facility management and external environment facility management factors will influence property consumer individual house purchase intention.

● The effects of in-store shelf design facility management factor influences consumer behavior

Can every store retailer's shelf design influence supermarket and large retail stores shoppers' behaviors when they visit the stores? However, currently many stores tend to build on traditional and repetitive design for their store shelf layout, it brings results in outdated store layouts.

Another important store shelf layout design aspect, retailer should consider carefully is the allocation of products on shelves. So, it seems that efficient shelf space allocation management does not only minimize the economic threats of empty product shelves, it can also lead to higher consumer satisfaction, a better customer relationship.

Why does supermarket shelves design is important? Any retail tore will sell product category within a shelf. They can use the same nominal category , e.g. crisps next to light crisps, same food product shelf. Anyway, a goal-based shelf display can contain several product, that determine a common consumer goal, e.g. fair trade. Hence, these two categorical product structuring methods are also described in terms of how to put product, or food on shelf benefit and attribute -based product categories.

These shelf design food or product storing method will have more influence consumers to choose to buy the supermarket or retail store food or products more easily , due to products, or food put on their shelf very convenient and systematic to attract consumers' shopping consideration to the supermarket or retail store.

● Music (FM) environment influence consumer consumption desire

Is it possible that shop music (FM) environment can raise consumer purchase desire? In one shop or supermarket, it can provide soft music (FM) equipment to let consumers can listen soft music or songs in the supermarket or retail shop when the are staying to spend more time shopping and whether soft music facility can be expected to raise customer individual value-added options to the music facility shop in the supermarket or retail shop.

Can the music facilities prolong consumers to stay in the store? It is possible that tempo soft music can influence consumers to stay longer time in restaurants and supermarkets and retail shops. It is possible that the different types of music (FM) in any supermarket, restaurant, retail shop owning music listening facility shopping environment. It will have possible to influence consumers to prolong staying in their shops. For example, one wine selling retail shop has classical music (FM) listening equipment to let consumers to listen when they enter the wine shop, it is possible to cause consumers to choose to buy more expensive wine products. Some researchers indicate when the wine shop owns classical music facility to let all consumers can list classical music when they walk in the wine ship, it can evoke the wine consumers to choose to buy purchasing higher prices wine products in the long term classical music listening environment. Otherwise, in a fitness sport center, musical fir and excite or popular music (FM) environment can attract fitness sport players' emotion to play and kind of fitness sport facility longer time. Also, in one supermarket, the soft music facilities listening environment can persuade or attract food consumers to spend more time in the mall consuming food or beverage also purchase other products more easily, due to they will listen soft music to be influenced to choose to prolong staying time in the supermarket. It seems that it has relationship between retail shop's music facility environment and consumer's emotion will be influenced by these different kinds of soft music or songs to raise consumption desire in the supermarket, if some consumers like to prolong to stay longer consuming time in the owning music facility environment's retail shop.

In fact, some researchers indicate the owning background music facility selling environment's ship , it can affect consumer decision making, memory, concentration consumption desire. So, classical , jazz soft music facility ought be installed in restaurants, retail shops, restaurants' environment. Otherwise, popular , exciting, noise, pop music facility ought be installed in fitness sport centers, theme park entertainment parks business places in order to influence fitness sport players or theme park entertainers to prolong playing or entertaining time to feel real sport or entertainment theme park playing machine facility's entertainment enjoyable feeling as well as attracting restaurant or supermarket or retail shop's consumers to prolong their staying time to make consumption decisions. Hence, it seems that music facility environment can raise consumers' consumption desire in possible.

● University bookstore atmospheric factors how to influence student's purchase book behavior?

Any university bookstore how to do international control and structuring of book internal environment to raise students' purchase book desires in university itself school's bookstore, it will be one popular question to any universities. Hence, whether the university bookstore internal (FM) factors include: lighting, music, colors, scents, temperature, layout and general cleanliness as well as university external factors include: the university bookstore shape/size, windows, university parking facility for students availability and location, which can play an influential role of the university bookstore image in order to influence the university itself students to choose to buy books from themselves bookstore or university outside bookstores.

Whether the university student needs to spend how long individual learning time and how much learning nervous to spend time to choose any kinds of book in the universiity bookstore or outside bookstores, this issue , he/she will consider. Because he/she does want to expect spend much time and nervous to choose to buy books in any bookstore. If the university's bookstore physical location and internal (FM) image can let its target student customers to feel it's all book products are stored in any attractive internal book shelves places, e.g. the cheapest and the most expensive different subjects of text books are stored in one system method to bring the positive image of value and quality in order to let university target student customers can find their books' choice location to spend less time to search any books to read in the unviersiity bookstore easily.

However, due to learning time is shortage to every university student of the university's book shelves can display all text books in the attractive right locations in the university bookstore as well as the university's bookstore ought has an adequate space to let university students to walk to anywhere and find any subjects of text books and compare their book sale prices in the bookstore's any shelves' locations easily when they walk to the subject of book shelf location, then they can make accurate decision either to buy the right kind of subject book or not buy it to read in the short time. They will feel their book choice purchase decision making process won't influence their learning time in themselves universiity. Then, the university students will be influenced by themselves university's bookstore's attractive external university facilities in the university's any teaching places and the university's bookstore internal attractive environment facility image which can influence the students to make final choices to buy their liking books to read from their university's itself bookstore. Hence, the university's bookstore internal and external building environment (FM) design factors will influence its students whether choose to buy from themselves bookstore or another outside general bookstore.

● How and why does retail atmospheric environment influence consumers behavior in retail shop?

Any shop's internal facility management design can influence atmospheric environment to influence consumer individual shopping desire, e.g. colour, lighting, music, crowding, design and layout factors, which internal shop (FM) environment can influence the first time shopping visiting client ' cognitive process how to feel the shop store image. Such as if the store's (FM) environment can bring enjoyable and fun and happy image to let them to feel shopping's enjoyment.

In conclusion, when consumers will like to stay longer time in the store. Due to the store's internal (FM) atmospheric environment can attract them to stay longer time in the store. Then, the customer's shopping value will raise and it can bring purchasing intention and shopping satisfaction. How can (FM) influence retail atmospheric physical (FM) environment ? Can (FM) bring indirect relationship to influence how the consumer individual causes positive or negative purchase intention when he/she has influence to prolong staying desire in the store, when the shop has good (FM) , it will bring long time to make consumption chance in the shop.

● Facility management influences
consumer satisfactory service
level

Can facility management (FM) quality influence consumer satisfactory service feeling? Any organization's facility management can improve the effectiveness of the maintenance organization. It can provide improved operational and maintenance functions to maintain the physical environment to support the overall mission. However, any organization will consider whether it improves its facilities, it will raise consumer satisfactory feeling when it provides the service to them, e.g. education service industry, when students need to often to attend any school's classrooms or lecture halls, computer rooms, libraries, all these facilities will be student's learning environment. If these school facilities can be maintenance to let students to feel comfortable to enjoy to study in their schools' any learning locations. Then, it has possible that to bring their enjoyable learning feeling in theirs schools.

● How school's facility management influences student's learning satisfactory feeling.

However, in education industry case, the school's facility management has those criteria can be used to measure effectiveness. Student individual response time between the student's request for computer use service in school computer rooms, library reading service in school library , classroom computer facilities and tables, chairs etc. furniture supplies service and the facility management supply number and available to useful time. If the student believes that the response time is too long when he/she feels need to use any school facilities, the actual number of seconds or minutes, he/she needs to wait how long time to queue to use his/her school's any facilities in library, classroom, computer room. So, the student's queue waiting time to use any his/her school's facilities, it can measure the school's facility management effectiveness.

● Scheduling of preventive maintenance activities.

It schedules of any maintenance activities are not arranged effectively to the school. Then, it will influence students' poor learning facility service to their school. For their situation, when the school's first floor has two men toilets are damaged. They are needed to be required. However, it is one week period, the first floor 100 students can not use the first floor men toilets. Hence, in this week, all 100 students need to go to other floors toilets to often use. They will feel busy and time is not enough when they need to attend to any classrooms to listen the first floor classrooms teachers' lesson. If he/she arrives the first floor classroom too late, due to he/she needs to go to another floor male toilets to queue to use. Then, he/she will feel angry and worries about whose absent or late attending classroom behavior when the lesson's teacher has attended early in the first floor classroom , and he teacher will need him/her to explain why he/she will go to this classroom lately, if his/her explanation won't be accepted to attend to the first floor classroom too late in the week. So, arrangement maintenance schedule to any school's facilities issue is importnt to influence student's satisfactory feeling to the school. Also, lacking of preventive maintenance activities will bring results in unscheduled shutdown of critical equipment can have an unrecoverable impact on the school's good learning environment providing to student's mission.

In fact, however in any organizations, such as school, ship, office etc. organizations, achieving balance of effectiveness and efficient difficulties and takes time and effort on the part of management and staff. It is not enough to establish an optimal relationship between these two parts. It has another factor that organizations need to consider costs. In today's budget tightening environment, decreasing expenses requires accepting a lower level of efficiency and effectiveness. The goal is to determine the point at which decreasing efficiency and effectiveness is no longer acceptable before that point is reached.

It brings this question : How to apply facility management knowledge to rise efficiency and effectiveness in order to improve quality standard of service to satisfy consumers' needs in short time? Such as school's facilities service case. What factors can influence student's level of satisfaction with regards to higher educational facilities services? It seems that any school's facilities will influence its students how to satisfy its education service indirectly. Because they need often to go to school to learn. So, any school's facilities, e.g. classrooms, computer rooms, libraries, toilets, lecture halls, canteens, sport and entertainment centers, research laboratories, school car parks, student enquiry counters, all these places to the school's any students will attend. So, how raise schools' facilities improvement to satisfy students' learning needs in the school's any locations which will have help to influence it student individual satisfaction level to the school's service, instead of every teacher individual teaching performance service to the school's students.

For any service organizations , such as hotels, restaurant, financial institutions, retail stores and hospitals etc. The physical environment can influence how customers' evaluation of their service. Due to service has intangible nature, so customers will rely on evaluate service quality.

Any higher education institutions are education service providing organizations. They need have comfortable and enjoyable educational environment to be provided to the students to attend the school's any places in order to meet whose learning expectations and studying experience needs. So, the school's facility management will be one factor to influence student's learning satisfaction when they expect to attend the school's any locations or places to let them to feel the school's learning environment have good facility management feeling.

In fact, if the school has comfortable classrooms or lecture halls educational environment to let its students to feel, it will bring assistance to raise their learning satisfactory feeling. So, comfortable learning facility management environment is one kind of school's facility service characteristics, it includes intangibility, perishability, inseparability and variability. So, they are every student individual learning feeling when they are attending to the school's any learning locations. So, school's facility management service feeling will influence whether they expect to choose this school to study. If the school's facility management learning environment is more comfortable and teaching facilities are better to compare other schools' facilities. Then, it will have possible to attract many students to choose this school to study. Such as any educational organizations, instead of the teachers (lecturers and professors) whose educational level is influence students number. The university's building environment will influence students' learning feeling, when they attend in the university. The facilities include laboratories, lecture theatres an offices, but also residential accommodations, catering facilities, sports and recreations centers because university students need have university life feeling to let them to fell the university can give welfare services , e.g. medical services, career guidance, sport entertainment, residential accommodation etc. service, instead of educational learning service in classrooms and lecture theatres. Hence, university's diversification facilities services are needed to satisfy university students to choose it to study, instead of university teacher's educational performance.

When one student can enroll the university to study from secondary education institution. The admitted student will usually consider two aspects to decide to choose the university to study. One aspect is the academic programs, of sequence of courses choices and the another aspect is the university's facilities whether they can satisfy their university life need, e.g. library, dorms, bookstore, food canteen , gym's sport entertainment, education technological facilities in the classrooms and lecture theatres to let the students to feel the university's teaching facilities are achieved his/her learning demand.

So, these two factors (teaching and learning and facilities) are linked to each other to influence student's total school learning experience and attitude towards a particular institution and this is termed as value chain in the student's learning process in the university. Hence, student individual evaluation variables will include teaching staff, teaching method, enrolment and facility enough supply actual service need.

However, the university's facilities, such as any residential accommodation, canteen, library , classroom, lecture theatre, sport gym, entertainment center will be their useful facilities need to satisfy their learning, entertainment and eating ,even living need in residential accommodation in the school's learning life experience every day. If one student chooses to live in the university residential accommodation . All of his/her learning and eating and living time and spending will be calculated to the university's any facilities to let him/her to feel it can provide enough facilities to let him/her to enjoy.

Hence, the facility management factor, such as overall campus environment, library, laboratory, classroom, lecturer theatre size and facility supply of on campus accommodation, welfare right service, parking areas, cafeteria , sport center etc. They will be every students facilities service needs from the university supplies choice. So, any university ought not neglect how to improve itself university's space area facilities to achieve satisfy their needs after they choose this university to study. Hence, any university's facility management will influence how the student's satisfactory learning service feeling when he/she chooses the university to study.

In conclusion, better facility management will attract more students to choose the university to study. Otherwise, worse facility management will not attract more students to choose to study the school. Hence, it seems that the school's facility management factor has relationship to influence student's satisfactory feeling, instead of teacher individual teaching performance factor to the school.

● Property facility management influences householder buying behavior

One new property's low price is attractive factor to influence property buyer individual preference choice. Does the new individual's facility management factor influence the property buyer's preference choice decision, if the property buyer feels its facility management is better than other similar properties, even it's price is higher than other properties. I shall indicate some cases to analyze this possibility as below:

Some properties' facility management service quality has possible to create true value for any property buyers when they consider the calculation ingredients to make decision whether to new property has higher value to choose to buy. The factors may include: price, natural environment, transportation tools convenient available, shopping centers supplies, the neighour quality, and the property's internal facility management etc. factors.

In fact, car or house purchase buyers, they have similar behaviors. It is that car's buyers will consider the car's machines whether they are safe to drive on roads, instead price, manufacture loyalty factors. It is possible that the car's machines quality factor will be preference to any car buyers when they make preference decisions to choose which brand its cars are the suitable. However, if the car's brand is famous and its appearance beautiful and price is cheap. But the car consumer feels its machine qualities are unsafe to let the driver to drive on road. Then, the car's poor machine quality factor will influence the car buyer's decisions to choose to buy this car. It can influence the car buyer individual car purchase decision.

The car buyer's behavior is similar to property buyer's behavior. Although, the new property price is cheap, good neigh ours are living near to the new property's location, shopping centers and transportation tools are available to near to this new property's area. But if the property buyers' feels its facility management is poor quality to compare other similar properties. Then, the poor quality of facility management factor will have possible to influence the property buyers whose final buying decision to choose to buy this new property. It brings this question: How and why can the facility management poor quality factor influence property consumers' preference choice?

In general, all property consumers won't know whether the new property's facility management is good or bad quality , they need to spend time to visit to the new property in order to observe whether its internal facility is satisfactory to his/her acceptable level. In simple, their purchase decision will regard to how to allocate household budget, how the household's economic resources are influenced, e.g. for travelling, visits to restaurants, comparing the different similar types of property product groups, e.g. apartments or houses or houses of a givn size data. For example, if one property's room(s) size is (re) small to compare other kind similar product type of room(s) size. Although the prior property's price is cheaper to compare to the later properties. But, if some property buyers hoped the property has large room(s) size, then the later larger room(s) size which will be possible to some property buyer's preference choice. Even, their property price is more expensive to compare the smaller room(s) size of properties. Thus, the property's room size which will be one major factor to influence property buyers' purchase decision. room's size had relationship to facility management issue. Moreover, if the room's quality and design is attractive, then it will bring more attractive to persuade some property buyers to choose to buy them to live in preference.

Hence, whether the new property is good durable product feeling which will influence householder's choice. If the householder feels the new property has long term durable life to avoid to spend much maintenance expense when they have been living in the new property for a long term period. They will believe it has better facility management, quality to let them to live longer time and the most importance is that they do not need to spend any maintenance expense , due to the property 's any internal facilities are damaged easily.

The external factors may include: culture, reference groups, family, social class and demography of lifestyle as well as internal factors may include: feelings, past property buying and living experience , property knowledge, motivation of the property buyer individual psychology. These both factors can influence any property buyer individual decision making process to do final house purchase behavior. However, internal factors, such as: property knowledge of facility management and property living experience, e.g. how to evaluate to choose to buy the property , due to the property buyer's past living experience for the past property's facilities whether its facilities can satisfy its property buyers' comfortable living needs. This internal factor will be more important to influence any property buyer's property purchase final decision. If he/she feels whose prior old property's facilities are satisfactory. Then, he/she will compare this new property and old property's facilities to decide whether this new property is value to buy. So, the old property's facility will be the measurement standard to compare his/her next new property purchase choice. So, the property purchaser will compare these new and old property's property facilities product knowledge to similarities among property alternative which will influence his/her final decision to choose to buy the new property to live.

It seems that property low price factor must not guarantee to attractive many property buyers' choice. Otherwise, it is assumed that many property buyers like rent or buy to live the property for themselves for long term intention. There are less property buyers expect to sell the first property to earn profit intention. So, they will usually consider whether the property is long term durable product to avoid to pay maintenance expense when they had been living in the property in long term.

Some factors that taking consideration are proximity to the specific location, housing prices, developer's brand, the payment scheme, reference group, which are not the main factors to influence any property buyer individual choice. Because property buyer's need is that the property has good facilities to supply to them to live, e.g. good heater equipment can provide hot water to them to bath in winter or good air conditioners can provide cold temperature to let them to feel cool comfortable feeling in summer in their homes. Good electric tools facilities , when they have need to use electricity in safe environment at home, e.g. car park accessibility facility , level of security facility , surface area facility and housing types, bedroom, bathroom facilities, quality of housing manufacturing raw material, house design , house durable guarantee, speed of complaint responsiveness, specification accuracy, confirmation of building plan service, showing legal file property purchase process service, finance instalments process assistance, speed of responsiveness, officers' skills of presentation. All of above these concern property facility management issues will influence any property buyers' final choice to decide whether the property is value to buy. So, facility management will influence property purchaser individual final decision in possible.

● Hotel facilities influence hotel consumer choice

Travellers choose hotel to live. They will consider price, room comfortable feeling, hotel location , gum sport or entertainment service facility supplies , hotel room booking service etc. factors to decide whether the hotel can achieve every traveller individual minimum living need. However, whether hotel facilities factor will be the main factor to influence travellers' living needs. How and why do travellers consider hotel facilities whether are enough supply or facilities of quality to satisfy their demand to cause their living choice to the hotel final decision.

Usually, hotel's customers won't plan to live too long time, e.g. more than three months in the hotel. Because they are travelling aim. It will bring this question: Does hotel facilities quality consider to influence their hotel living choice if the traveller is short-term traveller to the country? However , some travellers who have effort to spend money to live high class hotels, even their journey is short trip. Hence it seems that short trip , hotel living reason can not influence the high class hotel travellers' living comfortable demand to the high class hotel room. Hence , the high class hotel room's facility management quality is also needed high performance. Even, when they need to eat breakfast, lunch , dinner in the high class hotel canteens or playing any sport equipment, or gum equipment or wathching movie in the hotel's small cinema room . They must need high class hotel can supply more entertainment, restaurant , sport facilities to satisfy their comfortable needs in the high class hotel. Moreover, they must consider safety issue when they are living in the high class hotel. So, thy must demand the hotel have enough five fright equipment in their rooms, or corridors and the stairs to let them can leave the dangerous locations to arrive the most safe locations immediately when the hotel has fire accident occurrence in any where . So, it ensures that the high class hotel's customers must ensure the high class hotel's facilities can satisfy their any one of above these needs before they decide to live this high class hotel.

In fact, high class hotel's room price must be more expensive to compare the low class hotel. So, it explains why high class hotel's consumers will need the hotel has safe and good quality of facilities to let them to feel it is one reasonable price, safe , good service and good facilities' high class hotel to live. Usually, when the traveller arrives the country to travel, the travelers chooses the hotel to live, it is whose first time visit in common. So, he/she ought consider that the hotel environment seems it is good or bad to let the traveller to select to live. If the hotel's facility environment is new and beauty and design colorful to let the first time travellers to feel. Then, it is possible that good facilities environment can influence the first time travellers to select to live, even the hotel's room price is more expensive to compare other similar hotels in the travelling living places. Hence, it explains why hotel facilities can influence traveller individual room booking choice. When he/she is the first time to visit the hotel to select whether to live or not.

● How and why facility management can influence workplace productivity to bring customer satisfaction

Facility management is one part of manufacturers or retailers as their productivity in workplace as their input and functionalistics within physical environment. In fact, facility management in workplace may include: site selection, property disposal, site acquisition, workplace space allocation, space inventory, space forecasting facility management, interior furniture change planning, interior furniture installation, moving maintenance, inventory, design evaluation, employment satisfaction evaluation plan, external maintenance and breakdown maintenance, preventive maintenance, landscape maintenance, energy space facility management, hazardous waste disposal, capital , operating furniture budgeting. So, it seems that one workplace considered whether the workplace's facility is enough to let employees to work in order to raise efficiency and improve productive performance more easily. Then, it will bring this question:

● How and why workplace facility management can influence consumer individual satisfaction?

Strategic FM delivery is essential for business survival. I shall explain why for delivery is important to influence customer satisfaction. In business process view point, an effective and meaningful service to their customer , i.e. the user. For logistic industry, the product's delivery time will influence when the product can be sent to the user's arrival destination. If the product is delayed to sent to the user's home or office or any location destination. The reason is because the logistic product sender has no efficient facility management (FM) arrangement in its warehouse . Then, its warehouse lacks efficient (FM), which will cause users to feel its delivery service is poor and they will complain its delivery service staffs. Then, they will find another delivery service company to replace its service. So, it explains that logistic industry's warehouse (FM) service arrangement can raise efficient time to send any products to their customers in order to let they feel satisfactory service. For example, Amazon online logistic company's warehouse has applied artificial intelligence robotic tools to assist warehouse workers to arrange the different kinds of products to deliver to the right shelves . Then, the warehouse robotics will follow their right product shelves locations to follow the right products to deliver to US domestic or overseas product buyers in the short time and it can avoid the wrong products to deliver to the wrong buyers' risk. Also, the (AI) delivery tools can raise time efficiency to assist Amazon warehouse workers to reduce their work load, and tried to work in large warehouse environment. Although, its warehouse's area is large, the (AI) tools facility can help them to deliver the different products to different shelves in the right locations , e.g. exact product number and the kinds of product to be delivered to the right country' client's shelf location in the warehouse. Also, it implies FM is very important to influence Amazon warehouse delivery efficiency and avoiding delivery wrong occurrence chance. For example, the shelf location belongs to US domestic customers, or the shelf location belongs to Japan customers, or the shelf location belongs to Hong Kong customers, or any other Asia or Western countries' different customers' locations. The warehouse's facility needs have different countries' shelves enough space to put and it also need enough space to let the (AI) tools, robotic delivery workers and human workers both to walk to different shelves locations easily and the different countries' shelves number needs to be calculated accurate. For example, it has how many client number will buy Amazon's the kind product per day. If it has above 5,000 to 10,000 China clients to buy the kind of product. Then, it will need to make judgement how many shelves are placed in the warehouse. So, it can avoid to lack enough shelves to put any different kinds of products to prepare to delivery to China clients in efficient time and it won't avoid to delay to deliver to their homes or offices or any locations in China.

Hence, such as Amazon logistic case, it explains why warehouse's space shelves number and area or locations facility management can influence workers or (AI) delivery tools how to move convenient and avoiding the delivery to the customer's wrong destination chance occurrence and shortening time to deliver products to its clients efficiently. Then, due to the delivering time is shorten and the wrong delivery destination's occurrence chance is also reduced , even it can avoid to deliver the product to wrong client's destination occurrence. Then, the logistic firm's clients will feel more satisfactory to its product sale delivery service and their complaints will be avoided. Hence, it explains effective warehouse (FM) space management service arrangement is essential to any logistic businesses nowadays.

● Facility management brings departmental benefits

Why do organizations need have facility management (FM) service? As above examples indicate that (FM) can improve workplace environment facilities, e.g. warehouse environment to let workers to raise efficiencies or improve performances, even it can influence consumers to raise satisfactory to it's services indirectly, also it can help organizations' equipment to be used long term to cause old and are needed to spend expenditure to maintenance or change new equipment in order to improve better quality . So , it can assist organizations to avoid to spend more expenditure for new equipment purchase or maintenance. All these issues will be facility management service's benefits to an organizations, which can concern raising customers' service satisfaction, raising efficiency or improving productive performance, raising productivity, reducing equipment or property maintenance or new alternation much of expenditure spending, office or warehouse or any workplace space planning arrangement .

However, every organization will need a facility manager or manage whose team effectively . When a facility manager begins to apply FM techniques to solve business problems. The case for FM is made. It is a simple matter of demonstrating a qualified return on the investment required. Every organization's success, FM operation of three key activities: they include: needing a proper understanding of the organization's needs, wants, drivers and goals and knowing when needs to review its changing circumstances, developing an effective facilities solution o support the organization's needs, wants , property drives and contribute to achieve its goals both short term and long term, achievement of reliable delivery of that solution in a managed, measured manner.

So, it bring one question: What are the influential factors to be followed the right direction to FM manager's strategic FM operational decision? The influencing factors may include: ownership, governance sector, complexity and perhaps of most significant, the size of the organization's property portfolio.

In fact, major occupiers feel FM service need, they are large corporate organizations and public service organizations. Their aims usually are to raise. The most marginal improvement in efficiency or effectiveness, these aims are the great significance. Major property occupiers will already have a facilities department or individuals performing the FM function with another department like property, finance or human resource, sale and marketing's facilities.

Usually these FM need occupiers who will encounter this problem: How can apply FM service systems and processes to be developed to improve reliable service delivery making use of the economies of scale, not suffering because of the size of the problem. This question will be facility manager individual concerning question: How to apply (FM) technique to solve the improvement reliable service delivery making use of the economics of scale problem for whose organization?

In reality much of external facilities management benefits to organizations, instead of raising efficiency, improving performance, raising productivity, reducing maintenance expenditure, e.g. energy saving, reducing natural resource waste, increasing local employment, improving supply chain management are all elements of the FM contribution to every organization's need. Hence are the work life balance argument and provision of an effective and safe working environment that supports why some organizations feel need (FM) service to support their organizational development.

Moreover, on cost benefit of space saving efficient view point, space service cost reduction is a key driver for all organizations and the medium, or large sized players will benefit directly from a well coordinated facilities strategy. For example, application FM technique to help warehouse or office space area to save 50% space vacancy to let employees can move easily or putting enough furniture or equipment or many stocks can be putted in warehouses . So, paying more rent expenditure to rent or purchasing another new warehouse or office to satisfy workers or employees' working environment to be better need. If the organization has effective (FM) technique, then it has enough space vacancy to supply to the increase stocks number to be putted inside in warehouse and it can let workers to move safety in available to let staffs to move easily and equipment have enough space to be stored in the limited warehouse space problem.

For greater space savings benefits will bring either long term renting or buying of increasing offices or warehouse number expenditure problem to any organizations, when the organizations' cost or renting or buying accommodation probably accounting for 60 to 70% of total occupancy cost . So a strategic program to release space or the prevent the acquisition of moves can be the most significant consideration to any facility manager, with between 40% and 60% of the workplaces are unoccupied in most offices or warehouses at any given moment in time.

Hence, how to apply (FM) technique to save space occupied areas for employment moving or stocks or equipment saving need in offices or warehouses. This issue will be any facility managers' seeking methods to solve problem. However, the important major advantage of facility management to organizations is that the application of management principle to keep the organization's property assets with the aim of maximizing their potentials. Thus, any organizations' facilities have become important, due to the property facilities' worth will increase if the organization's facility management technique can protect the organization's facilities have good performance. Then, the organization's maintenance expenditure will reduce and it won't need to spend expenditure to buy any new facilities to replace old facilities , due to they often damage factor when they are used old.

In conclusion, it explains why effective FM combines resources and activities can raise work environment improvement, which is essential to the raising employee performance aim. For hotel living service case example, this industry must need have good facility management service because hotels must need to fully equipped in term and facilities for effectiveness to satisfy hotel living clients' demand , hotels ought need good facilities asset management style lead to effectiveness in service delivery, there are benefit derivable from the adoption of facilities management from which other hotels can learn from for their effective operations. Hence, it explains why effective FM can bring benefits to hotels' properties to be more comfortable, beautiful appearances to attract many hotel customers to choose to live the hotel. Because hotel's building industrial kitchens, rooms facilities, equipment , halls of categories, restaurant facilities, gum sport entertainment centers' facilities, fans, elevators, lifts, electrical installation, escalators, baking equipment, recreational facilities, including golf courses which will be important factors to influence hotel clients' comfortable living feeling, if the hotel can keep its all facilities in the best living environment often. Then, it can raise chance to attract many hotel customers to choose it to live. So , hotel industry has absolute need to implement effective FM strategy to keep its properties more attractive to satisfy its clients' living needs.

Instead of hotel industry, logistic transportation industry also needs effective facilities management in warehouse, because of the logistic company's warehouse 's facilities are good, then it will assist to raise employee individual efficiency in the safe and system shelve stored facilities in workplace environment and improving performance.

Consequently, it will bring the shorten time to deliver any products to clients to avoide the delaying time delivery in order to let customers to feel more satisfactory to their services. In simple, it seems that some industries need have effective facilities management techniques to help them to bring long term customer satisfactory feeling, worker individual efficiency raising and performance improvement benefits. Hence, it seems facility management techniques' demand will be increased to some industries in popular in the future because it has help to raise employee individual efficiency , productive performance and client individual satisfactory level consequently.

Facility management how influences employee Psychology to raise productive efficiency

● How to impact of workplace
management on well-being and
productivity

In facility management strategy, design can lead promotion, the value of offices that are enriched, particularly including warehouses, shopping centers to raise their market value. Moreover, effective organizations, such as raising powering workers when giving the effective design of office space. I assume that a good design of an interior office workspace environment seems a psychological department to influence staff individual emotion to bring positive power in order to raising productive efficient influence, such as in a commercial city office. So, it brings this question: How workspace management strategy can impact on staff's working behaviors in office.

In fact, office tasks general include various forms of productivity, e.g. information processing, information management and any clerical tasks by computerization. Hence, office productivity concerns how to influence each office white color worker applies computers to work in office. The office space can impact on white color workers' performances in these several aspects: feeling of psychological comfort, organizational physical comfort and job satisfaction and productivity, efficiency. So, it seems that office workspace design strategy can influence white color workers' working behavior and attitude and performance indirectly.

The office space management includes: how to removal from the workspace of everything except the materials required to do the job at hand, how tight managerial control of the workspace, and how to implement standardization of managerial practice and workspace design. So, these key ideas will influence how each white color worker's efficiency and productivity in office working environment.

For this office space design situation, a large unseparated small space size's space design can accommodate more people and so brings itself to economies of scale. As a result, space occupancy can be centrally managed with minimal disruptive interference from office workers. Indeed, many businesses now adopt a clean and fresh air office working policy because they have more employees than they have spaces at which they can work. This desks are either taken on a first -come first -served basis. (hot desking) or can be booked in advance. So , when a company has many employees need to work in a small space working environment. It must concern how to let staffs to feel more comfortable in order to reduce high psychological pressure to work in this uncomfortable working environment. Hence, it explains why workspace design can impact on office workers' performance in some offices. All these issues are assumed that empowering workers to manage and have input into the design of their own workspace, then the effective office or any working places space management will enhance wellbeing to bring workers' positive emotions and improving productivity. I also assume the space working environment design have relationship of these depend variable factors to influence office worker individual productive efficiency. The variable factors may include psychological comfort, organizational comfortable, job satisfaction, physical comfort and productivity.

However, office furniture , facilities will influence office white color workers' performance ,e.g. the room size whether is big or small for manage office worker, a high backed, comfortable leather chair is needed for office staffs to sit down to let more comfortable, the door and most of the walls need glass, the office room environment needs have sea-grass rug beneath the desk covering the immediate working area, the office also needs have plants and pictures, mail boxes, telephone and computer facility is needed. When one staff needs to send email or phone call or send letters or deliver documents conveniently. These office elements are essential in order to increase physical well-being and feeling of satisfaction to white-color workers. Hence, geren office and office working space design management is needed in order to influence white color workers' productive efficiency in long term.

● Effective workspace design can influence communication to raise productivity

Office white-color workers often need communication between their managers, supervisors, and themselves. Office communication extends from the way that a user experiences a service. An effective office communication can bring these benefits; Providing positive influence on decision making by presenting a strong point of view and developing mutual understanding, delivering efficient decisions and solutions by providing accurate , timely and relevant information, enabling mutually benefit solutions, building health relationships by encouraging trust and understanding between the high level, middle level and low level staffs.

Effective office communication needs to clearly communicate its nature and purpose. Good communication ensures that all service staffs are sending out the same messages. Communication is also important for ensuring the service understands what users requires and why he/she talks about understanding users' needs and communication receiver can have effective communication skill to understand what he/she needs the another to do and the another knows he/she ought how to work by his/her task demand. Then, it will shorten much time. If the office has 100 staffs need to often communicate. However, if the office has good space management arrangement to let every staff can communicate easily and walks to anywhere to find the right staff to communicate conveniently. Then, they can spend less time to waste on communication issue. Then, their productive efficiency will be also influence to raise.

● Health and safe work environment influences productivity

Is a health and safe work environment can raise employees' work productive efficiencies indirectly? How and why it can influence employees' productive performance? Some occupations' working environments are easier to occur occupational accidents and diseases risks when the workers are working in the high health and safe risk's working environment. Hence, health and safety issues at these high life risk workplaces can be considered as a key to influence employees' overall performance. The idea that health and safety management program have positive impacts on productivity.

When one worker needs to work in this high risk of health and safe workplace. He/she will consider whether how his/her work behavior will bring suffer serious injuries for shorter or longer time from work related causes in possible. So, he/she will work carefully in order to avoid injuries occurrence chance. It is possible to influence whose work performance, low productive efficiency in order to avoid any occupational accident occurrences in the dangerous workplace.

If the employee feels danger when he/she needs to stay in the warehouses stable location to work often. Then his/her absenteeism day number will have increase, due to he/she feels that workplace accidents and occupational illnesses and can lead to permanent occupational disability, when he/she needs to attend the stable dangerous workplace to work in the warehouse. Hence, he/she will choose to apply holiday often in order to avoid injuries chance increasing when he/she needs to stay in the stable workplace location in the warehouse. It explains why companies increase need qualified, motivated and efficient workers who are able willing to contribute activity to technical and organizational innovations. So, healthy workers working in healthy working conditions are thus an important precondition for organization to work smoothly and productively. Hence, a health and safety workplace environment can bring these benefits to organizations as below:

It can prevent among workers of learning work, due to health problems caused by their working conditions, the protection of workers in their employment from risks resulting from factors adverse to health. The placing and maintenance of the worker in an occupational, environment adapted to his/her physiological and psychological, capabilities, mental , physical and social conditions of workplace and adequacy of health and safety measures are needed to any employees in order to bring positive impact not only on safety and health performance, but also productivity. However, identifying and quantifying these effects will difficult to be measured as well as the quality of a working environment has a strong influence on productive efficiency.

For one aviation air plane manufacturing factory, where workplace can environment will have high risk to occur occupational related accidents to cause employees' injuries. Hence, employees will be consider themselves safety when they need to work in high accident occurrence workplace. The bad consequence will influence such as absenteeism day number increases, leaving this kind of aviation air plane job of employees number increases, low productive efficiencies, due to there are many proficient experienced employees who choose leave this kind of high accident risk occupation.

Consequently, any high accident occurrence risk workplace environment , employers need have good safe and health strategy to let their employees have confidence to work in this kind of high risk accident occurrence workplace if they expect low productive efficiencies effect is caused by high accident occurrence risk workplace factor.

● Employee personal
empowerment factor influences
performance

Is empowerment one good method to raise employee himself/herself effort in order to improve productive efficiency in organizations. Empowerment often consists of support groups, e.g. management's effective leading or trainer's training, course educational opportunities. Employee self-management education may impact to improve himself/herself job performance, e.g. increased self-empowerment, self-management skills and job treatment satisfaction.

Only organization's empowerment strategy can lead every employee to through improvements in the employee individual decision making efficacy, improvement task performance behavior by reviewing whether what are the employee himself/herself errors when he/she encounters any job difficulties, after he/she reviewed his/her task error and his/her manager feels his/her performance can be improved. Then, it can enhance satisfaction with the employee and his/her manage relationship and better access and raising efficient performance in possible . Hence, empowerment can let every employee to discover whether what task related difficulties he/she faces or encounters every day. When his/her manager give ideas to let him/her to know how he/she ought review his/her task error in a supportive education working environment, it aims to let the low performance or low inefficient employees to increase confidence to continue work in the organization. So, the employee turnover number will decrease , if the inefficient employees can feel that they can attempt to solve their task-related difficulties successfully by themselves. So, empowerment can increase social support, leadership and advocacy development , it has resulted in greater employee individual performance psychological empowerment, autonomy and authority to let every employee to feel to achieve to improve themselves efficiencies more effectively in any organizations.

For hospital organizational efficiency measurement empowerment influence case, how empowerment can influence hospital's efficiency raising? Efficiency is one of the most important indicators of hospital performance evaluation. Why do some hospitals' efficiencies poor? It is possible that mis management of resources, lacking health plan packages, e.g. coverage of basic health insurance, poor quality of care service, more payment demand for out-of pocket payment , quality of primary healthcare , healthcare providers neglect to concern potentially about service efficiency issues.

In fact, low hospital efficiency is the major problem to influence patients number to choose the hospital's medical service, e.g. when the hospital often needs patients to queue to wait for doctor's care medical service. They need to wait on hour at least or more when the hospital has many patients are waiting for its medical service. Then, it will influence them to choose another hospital to replace it , if the hospital 's medical fee is cheaper and it does not need patients to spend long time to queue to wait its medical service. So, service efficiency is important to influence patients consumers' positive or negative feeling to choose the hospital's medical service. Even, the hospital's doctors are famous or they own many medical working experience, if patients often need long time to queue to wait its medical service . Then, it will cause its patients number to be reduced .

These are variable factors to influence the hospital's inefficiency. They may include old speed hospital information system and medical record documents based on inefficient input and output variables. Input variables may include the number of hospital admissions, the number of nurses and the number of available beds. The output variable may include average of length of stay and bed turnover interval inefficient paper document record in the patient record administrative department.

However, to evaluate the hospital efficiency indicators may include technical, scale and managerial efficiency the out-based data development analysis approach and the variable returns to scales assumption was used. Based on the out-input based approach (maximizing the factors of medical service production), to increase efficiency the organization should be increased outputs.

Hence, when the hospital has good efficient evaluation method to measure every staff's performance , e.g. ward administrative clerk, patient registration clerk etc. Then, it can base on an put-put based approach and assuming a variable return to scale, there is capacity to improve technical efficiency and managerial efficiency in these any hospital different administrative units without an increase in costs and use of same amount of resources in relation to technical efficiency and managerial efficiency and scale efficiency of hospital's administrative labour individual task.

In conclusion, factors, such as modification of managerial practices, use of modern technologies tailored to the cultural, political and formulation of clinical guidelines to standardize the medical processes in order to reduce medical errors and increase the empowerment of health care buyers (insurance organizations), length of stay, management hospitals by specialist managers, administrative requirement, full time hospital physicians, limiting the authority of decision makers in relation to the recruitment of staff in accordance with the needs of the hospital and optimal allocation of beds, conducting economic evaluations and the type of hospitals ownership had an impact on the hospital efficiency significantly. By increasing the number of beds the hospitals efficiency decreases. Otherwise, optimizing the bed size can increase hospital efficiency.

However, the important factor to raise hospital overall staffs efficiencies empowerment is needed to let every hospital staff to review whether why and how himself/herself error is caused and he/she needs to review his/her errors to avoid to be caused from any negligence again in order to avoid patients' complaints again or reduce the patients' complaint number aims. So, empowerment of staff himself/herself error review factor is one major raising efficient good method.

● How organizational facility environment factor influences new and old employees long term performance

In psychological view ,in any organization's environments, they depend on the types of social and physical environment factors to influence employee personal behavior how to be caused. How and why does the employee select to do whose behavior? If the organization's physical and social environment is better, then it may influence its employees select to work hard. It is possible to bring productive efficient raising consequence.

In fact, when one new employee enters the new organization to work, he/she needs to learn how to adapt to cooperate with the organization's old employees to work together. So, it explains how and why organization's physical and social environment can influence the new employee individual motivation of behavior to work. In regarding new employee individual behavior by new employer's culture expectations as well as new employees need to adapt of actions that are likely to productive positive outcomes and generally discard those that bring unrewarding or puniishing outcomes by new employer's treatment.

However, anticipated material and organization environment co-operation outcomes between the new employee and the organization old employees' cooperation, which are not the only kind of incentives that influence the new employee behavior of the new employee actions were performed only on behalf of anticipated external rewards and punishment from the new employer. In actuality, the new employee concerns considerable self-direction in the face of the new employer's organization's old employees competing influences. However, when the new employee has adopted an intension and an action plan. When, he/she works in the new organization for a period, he/she can't simply not back and visit for the appropriate performances to appear.

The new employee's new job goal will be motivated by enlisting self-evaluative engagement in activities rather than directly. By making self-evaluation conditional on matching personal new job standards, the new employee will give direction to his/her new job pursuits and create self-inventions to sustain his/her efforts for new job goal attainment. The new employee will select to do new task behavior to give him/her self-satisfaction and a sense of pride and self worth for the new job chance.

Efficacy beliefs also play a key role in shaping the new employees' behavior to do their tasks by influencing the types of new organization's activities and working environments, the new employees choose to set into any factor that influences the employee's choice behavior can affect the direction of employee personal career development in the new organization. This is because the organizational working environment influences operating in the employee how to select working environments continue to work. Thus, by choosing and shaping the new organization's working environments, new employee can have a hand in what they expect.

In conclusion, when a new employee chooses the new organization to work. He/she must need to adapt the organization's new working environment. If he/she feels difficult to adapt or accept to the organization's new working environment, then he/she will be influenced to work inefficient or poor productive performance , due to he/she feels unhappy to work the new organization's working environment and the new organization's manager will dissatisfy his/her performance and complain or give verbal warning to dismiss him/her. Then, it will bring the poor consequence to let the organization's inefficient productive performance effect. If many new employees feel difficult to adapt to work in the new organization. Then, inefficient productive performance will be influenced to keep a long term. So, it implies that the organization will need to change its organizational culture in order to let many new employees can adapt and accept this new organizational culture to work happily if the organization expects new employees work to raise productive efficiency successfully.

● Raising efficient and effective
interview psychological methods

In human resource department, interviewing and selecting the most right applicants to do different kinds of positions, it is one part of HRM function. If the interviewer need to spend more time to interview to decide whom is the most right applicant to do the position in one day, e.g. 50 at least , even more applicants number as well as he/she can also make the more accurate personal selection decision to choose the most right applicant to do the position after the interview day. Then, the interviewing process needs to be avoided to spend more time to choose the most suitable applicant to do the position within the day. It is difficult to judge whether whom ought be the most right applicant to do the position, if there are more than 50 applicants , they are needed to be interview in the day. The consequence will bring HR department can spend extra time to do the interview task, but it can have enough staffs and time and resource to do other urgent or important task at the interview day. It will bring this question: How to apply psychological method to raise interviewer's efficiency to shorten to spend extra time to do interviewing tasks ? I shall explain some psychological methods to attempt to let interviewers have more confidence to select the most right applicant in short time as below:

1. Behavioral interview skill

The interviewer can apply the actual behavioral interview method to let the interviewee to answer how he/she deals the matters, he/she feels that it is the best decision in order to judge and analyze whether whom applicant is the most suitable to be selected, e.g. describing the situation, he/she needs or the task that he/she needs to accomplish. The situation may be from a previous job, any relevant event, describing the action he/she took and be sure to keep the focus on him/her , e.g. discussing a group project or effort in the team; explaining what results he/she achieved, what happen? How did the event and what dis the applicant accomplishes? What did the applicant learn?

In the behavioral-based interview. the interviewer can need the applicant to attempt to explain examples clearly in order to judge whose analytical skill whether he/she is the suitable applicant to do the position. The interviewer may ask the applicant to identify some examples from whose post experience where he/she demonstrated top behaviors and skills that employers typically seek. To judge whether his/her examples should be totally positive, such as accomplishments or meeting goals, the other half should be situations that started at negatively , but either ended positively or he/she made the best of the outcome.

This behavioral interview test aims to review whether the applicant's every example answer, he/she can provide an appropriate description of how he/she demonstrated the desired behaviors. In the behavioral interview, the interviewer can attempt to judge whether the applicant has good imagine effort to mind any relatively small set of examples to respond to a number of different behavioral questions to satisfy the right example are applied to the right situations in the limited interview time. Hence, behavioral interview can let the interviewer to make more accurate analysis to judge whether whom applicant(s) has (have) good analytical effort to solve any work-related situational problems in the most reasonable way or attitude in order to select whom is the most right applicant to do the position.

2. E-mail interviewing in qualitative research

E-mail interviewing is another good interview method to select right applicant to do the managerial level position. E-mail interviewing can be in many cases a viable alternative to face-to-face telephone interviewing. Internet-based qualitative research methods may include online personal interview and virtual focus groups. However, it brings two questions: What opportunities and challenges does online in depth interviewing present for collectively qualitative data? How can in depth e-mail interviews be conducted effectively?

The applicant targets may be the top-level manager, advertising executive , sales manager, human resource manager etc. management position applicants. They need to answer any complex or difficult interviewing question by email in the limited time, e.g. how to solve one case study problem , how to give recommendation to solve the situation problem. The interview participants may be recruited by tool/method of psychological test questions, the interview questions may be interview guide in a single e-mail and follow yp, length of email data collection period may be up to 10 weeks, the number of e-mail or follow up exchanges may be several number. The electronic formal and require little editing or formation before the applicants are processed for analysis all e-mail interviewing questions. So, they need to answer any managerial case study problem in limited time. It is one good managerial interview test method to evaluate whether whom applicant has the best analysis effort in order to the managerial position, because they need to find the best solutions to give recommendations to attempt to solve any situational problems in any un predictive case study problems. For example, when the applicant or a focus group of discussion applicants whom need to spend the maximum half hours to give recommendations to discuss to solve one complex or difficult case study problem either between the interviewer and the another interviewee applicant or between the group of five to ten interviewees (job applicants) themselves. Thus, after the interviewer sent the one case study question to let the applicants to know by every email channel. The interviewer needs to judger whether whom one applicant or one of the focus group applicants their recommendations are the most reasonable to solve the case study managerial situational problem within half hour to one hour. Then, the interviewer can make more accurate judgement to select whether whom has the best analytical effort to do the managerial position.

3. The effectiveness of motivational interviewing for young or older adult applicants selection process

How can apply case management skills to be effective to prepare any interview motivation? How to do the most effective and efficient to meet the objectives of the interview? Some interview techniques used may vary the based on the individuals involved in the interview. For an interview with the young age applicant more require a different approach than an interview with a senior adult applicant. The following are one pointers to assist with preparing for the interview as below:

Knowing the purpose of the interview and what needs to be accomplished . What is the expected outcome? Gathering all forms that need to be completed or signed having the interview and making list of questions that need to be asked, knowing the key facts and topics to be discussed, during the interview. Gathering factual information that may be helpful. Opening mind is needed in the whole interview process. Making an appointment for the interview and arranging sufficient time to set fully participate in the interview. Taking notes during the interview, let the participants know in general terms the reason notes are being made and how they will be used, opening ended questions invite the applicant to provide more information usually begin with other words who, what, where, how, asking one question at a time and keeping wording simple and specific, defining any terms that may be unfamiliar to the applicant , giving the interviewing participants in the interview an opportunity to ask their one questions or to clarify anything that was discussed, closing the interview with a review of the information discussed and facts gathered, reviewing any follow-up that is to be done by the case manager or others involved in the interview.

In an efficient and effective interview, the interviewer needs have good body and spoken word communication to the interviewee or the position applicant. Because a good communication can reduce waste time or avoid the extended longer interview time if the interviewer can make good communication to impact good message to let the applicant to understand what is the mean to his/her interview question. What he/she wants to know, the total impact of a message includes ,e.g. 7 % verbal (words), 38% vocal /volume, pitch, rhythm etc. and 55% body movements (mostly facial expression). The interviewer's body and verbal behavior can make more clear message to let the interviewee(job applicant) to understand what answers are he/she wants to know mostly. Hence, an efficient and effective interview can let the interviewer to control and manage the whole interview to evaluate whether whom the applicants' answers or feedbacks are more reasonable to be acceptable to be better to compare other applicants to apply the position more accurately.

● What is efficient achievement of technological inputs factor in construction industry

What is organizational efficient raising actual mean? I shall indicate construction industry case to explain technological factor is the major factor to assist construction organization to raise efficiency. For construction industry example, improved productivity could be attributed to advances in and increased usage of information technologies, increased competition, due to globalization and changes in workplace and organizational structures.

For construction efficiency, the construction process can reduce waste in coordinating labor and in managing, moving and installing materials, loss avoidance. It can achieve efficient aim. The construction productive efficient concept can be defined efficiency improvements as ways to cut waste and labor. So, one construction organizational efficient achievement means that it implemented through the capital facilities sector, these activities would significantly advance construction efficiency and improve the quality, timeliness, cost effectiveness of projects in construction processes.

On construction industry technological factor influence hand, it can influence that construction productivity how well, how quality, and at what cost buildings and infrastructure can be constructed, directly affects prices for homes and consumer products and the robustness of the national economy. Construction productivity will also affect the outcomes of national efforts to renew existing infrastructure systems; to build new infrastructure for power from renewable to renew existing infrastructure systems; to build new infrastructure for power from renewable resources to develop high-performance " green building" and to remain competitive in the global market. If the construction organization expected to achieve effficient aim. It ought consider how to change in building design, construction and renovation and in building materials and materials recycling, will be essential to the success of national efforts to minimize environmental impacts, reduce overall energy use, and reduce greenhouse gas emissions.

However, construction industry analysts differ on whether construction industry productivity is improved by efficiency outcome. They indicate construction efficiency needs to reduce 25-50 percent waste in coordinating labour and in managing, moving and installing materials. This is the most minimum standard efficient achievement level to any construction organizations.

What are the factors influence efficiency to any construction organizations? An efficient construction task process is made possible by a range of information technological tools and applications, including computer-aided design and drafting, three and four dimensional visualization and modeling programs, laser scanning, cost-estimating and scheduling tools and materials tracking. So, high technological tool will assist to raise efficient construction process to any construction organizations. It can help them to shorten time and avoid materials waste and control cost effective estimation for any construction projects.

Effective use of interoperate technologies requires effective team cooperative processes and effective planning up front and this it can help overcome obstacles to efficiency created by process fragmentation. Interoperable technologies can also help to improve the quality and speed of any construction project related decision making, integrate processes, managing supply chains, sequence work flows, improve data accuracy and reduce the time spent on data entry, reduce design and engineering conflicts and the subsequent need for rework, improve the life-cycle management of buildings and infrastructure.

All of these factors will influence whether the construction organization can implement efficiency in success. For example, interoperable techcholgies include legal issues, data-storage capacities and the need for " intelligent " search applications to sort quickly through thousands of data elements and make real-time information available for on-site decision making. How to improve job-site efficiency through more effective interfacing of people, processes, materials ,equipment, and information. The job site for a large construction project is a dynamic place, involving numerous contractors, subcontractors, trades people and labors, all of whom must require equipment, materials and supplies to complete their tasks. So, they need to know how to manage activities and demands to achieve the maximum efficiency from the limited available resources. Time, money, and resources will have possible to be wasted when projects are poorly managed, causing workers to have to wait around for tools and work crews are not on-site at appropriate time or when supplies and equipment are stored in complexity or difficulty, requiring that they can be moved multiple time (time waste).

How to improve job site safety and improve the quality of projects, significantly cut waste? The use of automated equipment, e.g. for excavation and earthmoving operations, pip installation, concrete placement, and information technologies, e.g. radio-frequency identification tags for tracking materials personal digital assistants for capturing field data. These high technological tool can help any construction projects to raise efficiency to process improvements and the provision for real -time information for improved management at the job site.

Moreover, on mannal research and development tools hand, instead of data technological tools hand, any construction organizations also need to consider how to take a variety of forms: How to test field on a job site? How to arrange lecture shows in efficient way, seminrs, training and conference, and scientific laboratories time, human resource available arrangement, spending expenditure budget to finish. Moreover, effective performance mearements are enablers of innovation and of corrective actions throughout a construction project's life cycle. They can help any construction companies or organizations understand how processes led to success or failure, improvements or inefficiencies and how to use that knowledge to improve construction products , processes and outcomes of active projects.

The nature of construction projects, the industry itself, any construction organizations ought consider the construction working environment how to influence construction workers' emotions. For example, when the construction site is high levels, of noise, dust and airborne particles, adverse weather conditions,and other factors that can cause injuries and thereby reduce efficiency and productivity. New types of equipment can make an active physically easier to perform, easier to control, move precise , and safer for construction workers. Similarly, changes in materials can reduce the weight of construction components, make them easier to handle, move and install. Manufacturing building components off-site providers need more control conditions and allow for improved quality and precision in the fabrication of the component, One study that examined the relationship between changes in material technology and construction productivity based on 100 construction a related tasks, the study found that labor productivity for the same activity increased by 30 % at least when higher materials were used and labour productivity also improved when construction activites were performed using materials that were easier to install or were pre-fabricated. So, it seems material heavy can influence construction worker individual productive efficiency in site, if the material is higher , then the construction worker's productivity will be influenced to improve (Goodrum et al. 2009).

Thus, the factors influence construction organization's efficiency. It focuses on whether the construction firm applies how advanced construction technologies to assist its construction workers to work as well as whether its construction environment can let workers to feel safe to avoid life danger or accident occurrence. When the workers do not worry about whose life safety as well as they can apply advanced construction technology to assist them to work. Then, their productive efficiencies ought need to be improved easily. Thus, facility management and advanced technology will be the main factor to raise construction workers' efficiencies.